# Beginner's
# CZECH
## with Online Audio

T0275377

# Beginner's
# CZECH
## with Online Audio

## Iva Cerna &
## Jolana Machalek

HIPPOCRENE BOOKS
*New York*

For information, address:
HIPPOCRENE BOOKS, INC.
171 Madison Avenue
New York, NY 10016
www.hippocrenebooks.com

Previous edition ISBN: 978-0-7818-1156-9

ISBN 978-0-7818-1424-9

# Table of Contents

Audio files available for download at:

**http://www.hippocrenebooks.com/beginners-online-audio.html**

# Acknowledgements

This book could not have been completed without the help of many people.

We would like to thank Bill Boeder and Iva Čeledová for their assistance, advice and comments while writing this book.

We also wish to thank our husbands, Ken Machalek and Pavel Čerňa, for their support and suggestions.

Many thanks to all of our friends who have contributed their thoughts and ideas.

And finally, we thank Katalin Boros of Eurolingua for giving us the opportunity to publish "Beginner's Czech".

# Introduction

The rich culture and languages of Eastern Europe are unique, intricate and subtle, steeped in tradition by hundreds of years of history. But, since the Eastern European countries were closed societies for over 40 years under communist rule, little is known about them.

After the fall of the Iron Curtain a flurry of activity is being spurred throughout Eastern Europe by the desire to establish democratic institutions and free market economies. Firms from the West are exploring business opportunities and expansion into these virtually untapped markets. A fresh and beautiful land together with the rich and exciting cultural heritage of its people has opened up for tourists to explore.

As a result, EUROLINGUA was started in September, 1990 to meet the growing demand for Eastern and Central European languages and cross-cultural instructions. EUROLINGUA primarily serves tourists and business people who deal in international trade.

The passionate traveler would like to understand and enjoy the people and the customs of the country he/she will visit. For a successful international transaction the businessperson has to know the appropriate conduct in various business situations. Finally, basic information about the geography, history and politics of the country to be visited, together with some language knowledge will make anyone feel more at home.

These considerations have brought about this book, in the hope that it will become your friend and guide during your trip. The knowledge of customs, manners and some basics of language will help you discover more exciting things and make more friends than you have ever dreamed.

The book has two parts. The first part gives you information about the country (geography, history, economy, culture, customs and manners) and the second part consists of language lessons.

The language lessons are designed for the traveler and the non-specialist amateur. You will learn useful phrases and words for special situations and basic grammar hints. The lessons will not cover all grammatical problems, nor will they give a rich vocabulary for sophisticated conversation. Instead they will teach you enough to feel comfortable in a variety of situations, which you will find described here.

With this small, compact book you will have in your pocket a collection of bits of information, sufficient to carry out satisfying interaction with the people of the country you visit, in their own language. It is the result of many hours of work, research and travel done by enthusiastic teachers and travelers who wish you good luck in your study and a wonderful trip.

# Geography

The Czech Republic is situated in Central Europe, occupying an area of 30,450 square miles (78,864 square kilometers). It is an inland country bordered by Poland to the north, Slovakia to the east, Austria to the south, and Germany to the west. The country has two main parts: Čechy (Bohemia) and Morava (Moravia).

The terrain ranges from lowlands and uplands to hills and mountains. Geologically the mountain ranges of Bohemia and Moravia belong to the Hercynian Massif. The central lowland of Bohemia is surrounded by mountain ranges which create a natural border of the region. These mountain ranges include Jizerské hory and Lužické hory in the north, Krkonoše (Giant Mountains) and Orlické hory in the northeast, Šumava in the south, Český les (Bohemian Forest) in the southwest, and Krušné hory (Ore Mountains) in the west. The highest peak of the Czech Republic is Sněžka (5259 ft./1602 m) in Krkonoše. The uplands and mountains of Moravia create a natural transition to the Carpathians in Slovakia. The southern portion of Moravia consists of lowlands known for their agriculture.

The main rivers in Bohemia are Labe (Elbe) and Vltava (Moldau). Morava (Moravia) is the main one in Moravia. The Republic has only a few lakes, most of them are of glacier origin. The largest is Černé jezero in the Šumava mountains. However, there are a great number of ponds, especially in Southern Bohemia. Mineral springs are abundant. The most famous ones can be, of course, found in spa locations, e.g., Karlovy Vary (Karlsbad) or Mariánské Lázně (Marienbad), where the mineral water is used for health purposes.

The Czech Republic is located in a mild continental climate zone with predominantly westerly winds. There are four distinct seasons. Summers are usually warm and humid with rainfall. Winters are cold and humid. Mountains are snow-covered most of the winter, while lowlands get a mixture of snow and rain. Spring starts in March/April and Fall can come as early as at the beginning of September. The coldest month is January and the warmest is July. Temperatures can reach 89°F (32°C) in July and August and be below freezing in January.

The Czech Republic has a population of 10.4 million people. Given the area it occupies it results in a very high population density: 340 inhabitants per square mile. Most of the population consists of Czechs with a small percentage of Germans, Poles, Hungarians, and Slovaks. The highest concentration of population is in the industrial areas. The urban population is 79% of the total population.

Praha (Prague), the capital, with a population of 1.3 million is the largest city in the Republic. It is also the center of the political, economic, and cultural life of the country. The old sections of the city with famous historical monuments and sights make Prague one of the most beautiful cities in Europe. Other major cities include Plzeň (Pilsen) in Bohemia and Brno and Ostrava in Moravia.

The Czech Republic is a country with a strong industrial tradition dating back to the end of the 19th century. Industry is primarily concentrated in the cities and mining areas. Machine, textile and glass factories, and metallurgy are especially strong. Agriculture is concentrated in the central lowlands of Bohemia and in Southern Moravia. The main crops are wheat and sugar beets. Southern Moravia is best known for its wine production.

# History and Politics

The first significant inhabitation of the region of today's Czech Republic was by the Celts around 400 BC. Slavic tribes did not come to the region until the end of the 5th century AD. In 623 AD Samo, a merchant from an area of today's Germany, formed the first state in this region. It included Slavic and Celtic tribes. After his death in 658 AD the state disintegrated. Some of its lands were absorbed by the Great Moravian Empire (around 830-907 AD).

By the end of the Great Moravian Empire, the Přemyslid dynasty (Přemyslovci) had consolidated its power in Bohemia and, by the 11th century, their territory also included Moravia. The Přemyslid dynasty ruled until 1306. Wenceslas (Václav), one of the Přemyslid princes who defended the spread of Christianity, was assassinated by his brother. He was later canonized, becoming St. Wenceslas (Sv. Václav). A statue of him on a horse stands at the top of Wenceslas Square in Prague. In 1212 King Přemysl Otakar I negotiated the Golden Sicilian Bull, a document which made the Přemyslids hereditary monarchs of Bohemia and its territories. In 1306 the last of the Přemyslids, Wenceslas III (Václav III), was assassinated at an early age leaving no heir to the throne.

In 1310 John of Luxembourg (Jan Lucemburský) was chosen for the Czech throne. His son, Charles IV (Karel IV), was the first Czech king to also become a Roman Emperor. During his reign (1346-1378) Prague became the cultural, economic, and political center of the empire. Many gothic structures were built in Prague, among them the famous Charles Bridge and St. Vitus Cathedral at the Prague Castle. In 1348 Charles IV established Charles University, the first in Central Europe. When he died in 1378, the Czech state was one of the most powerful in Europe.

At the end of the 14th century, plague struck the region reducing the population by as much as 15%. At the same time hostility to the careless lifestyle led by the clergy grew throughout Europe. John Hus (Jan Hus), a professor at Charles University, criticized this kind of lifestyle. Soon the criticism shifted from a theological to a social dispute. Hus was arrested on behalf of the clergy and burned at the stake on July 6, 1415. This led to further civil unrest. The followers of Master Hus, called Hussites (Husité), on July 30, 1419 threw 12 city officials from Prague's New Town city hall windows. This was the start of the Hussite wars which ended in 1434 at the Battle of Lipany with the defeat of the radical Hussites.

Moderate Hussites made an agreement with the Roman Emperor Sigismund (Zikmund) which allowed the Czechs to choose their religious belief. By 1458 70% of the population belonged to other than Catholic religion. As a result, George of Poděbrady (Jiří z Poděbrad) was elected as the Czech king (1458-1471). He was succeeded by the Jagellon dynasty from Poland. In 1526 Ferdinand I of Habsburg became the Czech king. This was the beginning of Habsburg rule which lasted more than 300 years.

The Czech nobility who put Ferdinand I of Habsburg into power soon resented the constraints he imposed on their power and property. This escalated in 1620 with the Battle of White Mountain where the Czech nobility was defeated. The leaders of this movement were executed and any signs of Czech nationalism were crushed. The Czech language was suppressed and the Czech people were stripped of all power. This event was followed by massive emigration.

At the end of the Thirty Years' War, the Habsburgs managed to hold on to Bohemia where social and living conditions continued to deteriorate. This led to many uprisings. Maria Theresa of Habsburg (Marie Teresie) (1740-1780) introduced some social and economic reforms (e.g., a new school system and a stronger industrial base) but at the same time she continued dominance of Bohemia by the Austrians. She was succeeded by her son Joseph II (Josef II) (1780 - 1790) who in 1781 abolished serfdom and issued the Edict of Tolerance which ensured more religious freedom.

The end of the 18th century was the beginning of the Czech Renaissance when the Czech language and culture started to flourish again. In 1789 the first Czech newspaper was published and in 1818 the Czech National Museum was established. At the beginning of the 19th century Bohemia was one of the most industrialized parts of Europe. It had a dense railroad system and a strong industrial base. The most prosperous were metallurgy, machine, glass, textile, and sugar industries. At the end of the 19th century even some political freedom was gained. The Habsburg rule ended in 1918 at the end of World War I.

The 1918 Treaty of Versailles broke up the Austro-Hungarian Empire and freed both the Czech Lands (Bohemia and Moravia) and Slovakia, which then on October 28, 1918 formed a common state under the name of Czechoslovak Republic. Thomas G. Masaryk became the first president. During the twenties and thirties Czechoslovakia was a democratic state and was among the most prosperous countries in the world. The depression of the thirties and the later German invasion crushed the nation once again.

Czechoslovakia was betrayed at the 1938 Munich Treaty when its allies agreed to give the Sudetenlands to Hitler in order to prevent war. This was the first step toward the occupation of the Czech Lands by the Germans which began on March 15, 1939. Slovakia became a puppet state with a Nazi government. The assassination of R. Heydrich, the head of the German government in the Czech Lands, on May 27, 1942 resulted in the introduction of martial law and in the killing of all the men in the village of Lidice and the leveling of the village. On December 12, 1943 the Czechoslovak government in exile signed a friendship treaty with the Soviet Union. On May 9, 1945 the Soviet army liberated Prague from the Germans. Based on the Yalta Treaty, the American army was allowed to liberate only a small portion of Western Bohemia.

After World War II, Czechoslovakia attempted to continue its democratic politics under the presidency of Edvard Beneš. However, the Communist Party, which was established in 1921, won the trust of the war-exhausted population and by February 1948, headed by Klement Gottwald, held the reins of power. In June 1948, Gottwald became the first communist president. He had strong ties to Moscow and to his mentor Joseph Stalin. All ideas which did not agree with the Marxist-Leninist idealogy were forced underground. Czechoslovakia's strong industrial base started supplying factory machinery to the Soviet Union.

After the deaths of Stalin and Gottwald in 1953, communist rule continued. In 1960, a new constitution reaffirmed the dominant role of the Party and its Marxist-Leninist idealogy which had become the basis of the whole education system. During the 1960's a new generation of intellectuals started to question the principles of the Party. This escalated in the spring of 1968 under the leadership of Alexander Dubček when the liberals wanted to introduce "socialism with a human face." All hopes were crushed on August 21, 1968 when Czechoslovakia was invaded by armed forces of the Warsaw Pact. "Prague Spring" was followed by another massive emigration to the West.

The next twenty years can be characterized by economic stagnation and more oppressive government, especially under the rule of president Gustáv Husák. However, the hopes and ideas of "Prague Spring" were not forgotten. An underground movement called Charter 77, a group which was opposed to the abuse of human rights in Czechoslovakia, was founded by Václav Havel. The members of the group were prosecuted and Havel himself was imprisoned.

The rise of Solidarity in Poland and the election of Gorbachev to head the Soviet Union gave more strength to the anti-communist movement in Czechoslovakia. On November 17, 1989 a peaceful student march was stopped by a special police unit and the participants were brutally beaten. The Civic Forum was formed in opposition to the government. The nation responded with marches, a general strike, and demonstrations. The communist regime collapsed and Václav Havel became president of the country in December 1989.

After the "Velvet Revolution", a nationalistic movement began to flourish in Slovakia under the leadership of Vladimír Mečiar. The Slovaks wanted independence from the Czechs and that became a reality on January 1, 1993. Two new countries emerged from this peaceful split, the Czech Republic and Slovak Republic. Even though there are some political differences, both countries continue to pursue a market economy, but at their own pace.

The Czech Republic is a parliamentary democracy. The main political parties include: Civic Democratic Party, Civic Democratic

Alliance, Independent Democratic Party, Christian Democratic Party, Czech People's Party, Communist Party of Bohemia and Moravia, Republican Party, and Democratic Left Block. The elections are held every four years. The president is elected by the parliament.

# Business and Economics

After the Velvet Revolution in November 1989, the Czech Republic quickly moved toward establishing a Western type market economy. Several waves of privatization have occurred in the country since 1989. The first was the privatization of small shops and businesses (e.g., shoe repair, cleaners, carpentry). Later, bigger businesses and agricultural land were privatized. Many of the bigger businesses entered into partnerships with Western firms.

Unlike Poland and Hungary, the Czech Republic had no private enterprises prior to 1989. The Czech approach was a massive privatization. By the end of 1993 about 60% of large companies were in private hands. The Czech government decided to privatize most national assets by selling books of vouchers which every Czech citizen could purchase for 1,000 Kč. These vouchers could be used to bid on shares.

As a result, about 10 major mutual funds were established. Many people sold their books to these mutual funds for 10 to 15 times the original price. The funds acquired a very large number of vouchers, but they are not allowed to hold more than 20% of any company's shares. The shares are traded on the Prague stock market, which opened in the summer of 1993.

The Czech Republic offers one of the best investment opportunities in the former Eastern European block due to its close proximity to Western European markets, stable political situation, and historically strong industrial base. The Czech consumer market is growing fast and the inflation rate is relatively stable.

Foreign investment, labor, and bankruptcy laws are still changing (a new bankruptcy law came into effect in April 1993). Currently the standard foreign investment contract provides that investors cannot lay off Czech workers for five years. Prague has the lowest unemployment rate in the country. In contrast, the mining areas had in 1993 unemployment as high as 5%. Unfortunately, labor mobility is constrained due to limited housing, especially in Prague.

The United States has a strong economic presence in the Czech Republic. However, due to its location in Central Europe, the Czech economy is being integrated into the German economic sphere of influence. The main items imported into the Czech Republic from the United States in 1993 included: electronic data processing and telecommunications equipment, feedstuff for animals, pumps, measurement and analytical instruments, tractors, printing and bookbinding machinery. The United States imports from the Czech Republic included: glassware, footwear, textile and leather machinery, machine tools, vegetables, tractors, fabrics and textile materials, and rubber tires.

# Culture and Arts

The Czech Republic offers a rich cultural heritage seen throughout the country in its architecture, museums, galleries, music, literature, theater, and film.

## ARCHITECTURE

### 1.   Castles and Chateaux

Castles and chateaux are valuable evidence of the economic, technical, and cultural heritage of a particular era. The first fortified settlements were built in the 9th century during the Great Moravian Empire. The first stone castles, which mostly originated on the sites of old Slavic tribal castles, were royal castles built during the reign of the Přemyslid dynasty. With the establishment of the feudal system, castles were also built by the nobility and highest church officials. The builders used natural formations and various forms of architecture in their design.

Most of the older castles were reconstructed in the past, sometimes only a few elements represent the original style. It is not unusual to find several architectural styles combined into a harmonious art piece.

Romanesque style castles were built during the 11th-13th centuries. These structures were very simple, usually a castle-tower combination. Examples of castles from this period include: **Cheb, Loket,** and **Přimda** in Western Bohemia.

Gothic style castles were built during the 13th-15th centuries. These structures became more complex and included a palace, tower, and chapel. Examples of castles from this period include: **Bezděz** in Northern Bohemia, **Buchlov** in Southern Moravia, **Kost** in Eastern Bohemia, and **Křivoklát** and **Karlštejn** (the former place for protecting the coronation jewels) in Central Bohemia.

Renaissance style chateaux were built during the 16th century and at the beginning of the 17th century. These new structures replaced the cold stone castles. Defense systems (e.g., towers) lost their justification and disappeared. The structures were usually closed formations with four wings and an arcaded courtyard. Examples of chateaux from this period include: **Telč** in Southern Moravia and **Velké Losiny** in Northern Moravia.

Baroque style chateaux began to emerge during the 17th century and continued through the 18th century. Structures of this period had a three-winged ground plan and their interiors were more functional (e.g., library, theater, or gallery). Their immediate surroundings were landscaped into beautiful parks, gardens, and paths of access. The whole complex appeared harmonious, sensitive to the surrounding countryside. Examples of chateaux from this period include: **Český Krumlov** in Southern Bohemia and **Rychnov nad Kněžnou** in Northern Moravia.

Rococo and Classicism style chateaux were built in the 18th and 19th centuries. During this period chateaux began to lose their dominant role due to the arrival of capitalism. However, they were still built up to the early 20th century. Two examples of this style are **Veltrusy** in Central Bohemia and **Sychrov** in Northern Bohemia.

The Neo-Gothic style emerged in the mid 19th century due to the arrival of Czech nationalism and a return to the art of the Gothic era from the reign of Charles IV. Examples of chateaux built during this period include: **Hluboká nad Vltavou**, one of the most beautiful chateaux in the Republic, in Southern Bohemia and **Konopiště** in Central Bohemia.

At the beginning of the 20th century, several chateaux were remodeled in the Neo-Renaissance style. **Červená Lhota** in Southern Bohemia is an example of such structures.

## 2.   Prague

**Prague** (Praha) is told to be one of the most beautiful and best preserved historical cities in Europe.

It became the seat of the Czech princes at the end of the 9th century. Later on, it turned into an important trading town and the seat of the Czech kings. The real flourishing of culture, arts, and the economy began during the reign of Charles IV in the first half of the 14th century.

One of the best ways to see how history flows through the city is to walk the **Royal Route** from the **Old Town** (Staré Město) across **Charles Bridge** (Karlův most) to the **Lesser Quarter** (Malá Strana), and up the hill to the **Prague Castle** (Pražský hrad - Hradčany).

The tour starts in front of the **Municipal House** (Obecní dům) on the corner of Republiky Square and Na příkopě Street. The secessionist Municipal House (early 20th century) with its several concert halls and a ball room plays an important role in Prague's cultural life. From here you walk underneath the late gothic **Powder Tower** (Prašná brána) built at the end of the 15th century. The walk continues through **Celetná Street** lined with medieval buildings to the **Old Town Square** (Staroměstské náměstí).

In the middle of the square is the Ladislav Šaloun's **Jan Hus Monument**, set in place in 1915 to commemorate the 500th anniversary of the Hussite movement. The square is dominated by the gothic **Old Town Hall** (Staroměstská radnice) with its **Astronomical Clock** (Orloj) constructed by Mikuláš of Kadaň in 1410. On the east side of the square is the **Church of Our Lady Before Týn** (Kostel Panny Marie před Týnem), also known as **Týn Church** (Týnský chrám), the **Týn School**, and adjacent is the **House at the White Unicorn** (Dům U bílého jednorožce). The north side is dominated by the rococo style **Kinský Palace**, built in the second half of the 18th century, and the west side by the baroque **Church of St. Nicholas** (Chrám Sv. Mikuláše), built in the first half of the 18th century.

From the Old Town Square the tour continues through **Small Square** (Malé náměstí) where you should notice the **Rott's House** (Dům U Rotta). Here, in the 15th century, was located a printing press which produced the first Bible in the Czech language. From here the route winds through the medieval streets of the Old Town to the banks of Vltava River. Cross the river on the Charles Bridge built in the 14th and early 15th centuries (main architect Petr

Parléř). In the early 18th century baroque sculptures were added to the bridge, many of them created by Austrian sculptor Matthias Bernard Braun and Czech sculptor Max Brokoff. Both ends of the bridge are marked by towers: the **Lesser Town Bridge Tower** (Malostranská mostecká věž) built during the 12th-15th centuries and the **Old Town Bridge Tower** (Staroměstská mostecká věž) built during the 14th and 15th centuries.

Once in the Lesser Quarter, the tour continues through Mostecká Street to the **Lesser Quarter Square** (Malostranské náměstí) which is dominated by the baroque **Church of St. Nicholas** (Chrám Sv. Mikuláše) built by K. I. Dienzenhofer in the mid 18th century. From here take Nerudova Street up to the castle. Many of the buildings along this street are foreign embassies and consulates.

The **Prague Castle** complex, called Hradčany, offers a colorful combination of architectural styles. The castle was founded in the late 9th century and became the seat of the princes and kings. It was rebuilt in the Gothic style during the reign of Charles IV. Some of the original elements are still preserved beneath **Vladislav Hall** (Vladislavský sál). The castle was again reconstructed during the reign of Empress Maria Theresa in the Neo-Classical style in the second half of the 18th century. The **St. Vitus Cathedral** (Chrám Sv. Víta), that dominates the complex, was founded by Charles IV. Its construction started in 1344. First, French architect, Mathieu d'Arras, was in charge of the project. After his death the work was assigned to Petr Parléř of Gmund and his sons. Construction continued on and off for the next five centuries and was finished in 1929.

With the revival of Czech nationalism during the 19th century two important Neo-Renaissance style buildings were built in Prague: the **National Theater** on the bank of the Vltava River and the **National Museum** at the top of Wenceslas Square.

The post World War II era can be characterized by massive housing construction on the outskirts of Prague. Only a few new structures were added to the center of the city: the department stores **Máj** and **Kotva**, built by foreign firms, and the **New Scene Theater**.

## 3. Provincial Towns

Many architectural styles are preserved not only in Prague, but also in outlying areas. The towns of Southern Bohemia, e.g., **České Budějovice**, **Český Krumlov**, and **Tábor**, contain examples of Renaissance and Baroque style nobility houses in their town squares. West Bohemia spa towns, e.g., **Karlovy Vary** (Karlsbad) and **Mariánské Lázně** (Marienbad), contain representation of the Neo-Classical style with its arcaded colonnades and lavish spa houses.

## MUSEUMS AND GALLERIES

Almost every large town has a museum or civic gallery displaying regional civic traditions and folk art. Prague has several national museums and galleries. The **National Museum** (Národní museum) at the top of Wenceslas Square (Václavské náměstí) offers many biological exhibits from the country and abroad. The **Technical Museum** (Technické museum) displays the technological development of the Republic. The **National Gallery** (Národní galerie) has several locations: the **Sternberg Palace** (Šternberský palác) featuring old European and European art of the 19th and 20th centuries, the **Convent of the Blessed Agnes** (Anežský klášter) displaying collections of the 19th century Czech art, and the **Convent of St. George** (Jiřský klášter) showing the castle collection of old Czech art.

## MUSIC

The rich musical heritage of the Czech people is known all around the world. The most celebrated classical musicians include: **Bedřich Smetana** (1824-1884) with his operas *Prodaná Nevěsta* (The Bartered Bride), *Libuše*, and the six symphonic poems *Má vlast* (My Fatherland); **Antonín Dvořák** (1841-1904) with his *Symphony No.9 "From the New World"*; **Leoš Janáček** (1854-1928), with operas *Káťa Kabanová, Její pastorkyňa* and other symphonic works. The most famous foreign musician who lived and composed in Prague was **Wolfgang Amadeus Mozart**. Mozart first became famous in Prague with his opera *The Marriage of Figaro*. He later composed and premiered *Don Giovanni* there. Every large town has a symphony orchestra and local folk bands.

## LITERATURE

Writers and poets have always been held in high esteem by the Czechs. The most famous writers of the early 20th century were **Karel Čapek** (*RUR*) and **Jaroslav Hašek** (*The Good Soldier Schweik*), both wrote with anti-war themes. Another famous writer who resided in Prague, but wrote in German, was **Franz Kafka**. Because of the communist regime, several writers left the country and wrote and published in exile. This group is represented by **Josef Škvorecký** (*The Bass Saxophone*) and **Milan Kundera** (*The Unbearable Lightness of Being*). **Bohumil Hrabal** (*Closely Watched Trains*) and the Nobel Prize winning poet **Jaroslav Seifert** are representatives of the group that remained in the Republic.

## THEATER

Czech theatrical tradition goes back to medieval times when traveling theater companies performed throughout the country. But major expansion of Czech theater occurred at the beginning of the 19th century and continued at the end of the century with the construction of the National Theater. Prior to that, most plays were performed in German. Prague has many theaters which specialize in different performances. Besides the **National Theater**, which shows classical drama, ballet, and opera, several other theaters are worth visiting. The **Smetana Theater** performs opera and ballet; the **Tyl Theater** specializes in comedy and drama; the **New Scene Theater** shows contemporary comedy and drama; and the **Laterna Magika Theater**, a one of a kind, combines acting with audio-visual techniques. The most famous Czech contemporary playwright is, of course, **Václav Havel** (*The Garden Party*; *The Memorandum*), who in 1989 became president of the country.

## FILM

Perhaps the best known Czech movie directors are **Miloš Forman** (*One Flew Over the Cuckoo's Nest*; *Amadeus*) and **Jiří Menzel**, (*Closely Watched Trains*; *My Little Sweet Village*).

# Everyday Life

## ADDRESSING PEOPLE/INTRODUCTION

There are two ways of addressing people in the Czech language: formal and informal. You may address or greet a younger person or your friend in an informal way, e.g., ahoj, nazdar, or čau (all meaning "Hi"). If the person is older or somebody who you do not know very well, you would use the formal way to address or greet them, e.g., dobrý den (lit.: Good day), dobrý večer (Good evening). When you are addressing people who have a title, use it with the word Mr., e.g., Mr. Engineer (pane inženýre), Mr. Doctor (pane doktore). Fur further information refer to Lesson 1, paragraph 2.

## NAMES

Czechs have two names: first and last (family) name. Last names usually come in two different forms, male or female.

a)  Noun based last names:
    male:    Novák
    female:  Nováková

    Note:
    The fleeting "e" rule is in effect. The -e- is dropped in other than the nominative and vocative cases of masculine nouns.
    male:    Kubíček
    female:  Kubíčková

b)  Adjective based last names:
    male:    Starý
    female:  Stará

## ASKING FOR DIRECTIONS

When asking or giving directions instead of using compass points (west, east, etc.), directions are given by landmarks and right and left hand turns. For example, when asking how to get to a certain place one will get instructions in the following manner: make a right turn, then go to the train station and then make a left turn.

## GROUND TRANSPORTATION

### 1. City Transportation

Most of the bigger cities have good public transportation systems. Prague has an excellent system including bus lines, street cars, and a subway. The subway is an especially good way to get around town. It is a very clean and safe way to travel.

### 2. Taxi

Prague has good taxi service operating 24 hours a day. There are taxi stands at the airport, train stations, and the town center. In any other location you can stop a taxi by waving your hand. Check for the price in advance. Taxis are rare in smaller towns.

### 3. Trains

There are two kinds of trains: regular (osobní) and fast or express (rychlík). Two different classes (first and second = coach) are available on the fast trains. It is not necessary to buy tickets in advance. Seat reservations are usually required only on some routes and only in some cars.

### 4. Bus

While your travel plans may be restricted if you decide to travel by train, you can get to almost any place by using a bus. Since the number of seats on a bus is limited (only shorter routes allow standing while riding), it is a good idea to reserve a seat in advance if possible.

## 5. Car

There are no restrictions if you want to travel by car. The condition of the roads is not bad, but be aware of the fact that roads are narrow and most have only one lane in each direction. Traffic is normally not very heavy, except for Friday and Sunday evenings when people drive to and from their country cottages.

## 6. Car Rental

There are numerous car rental agencies. Hertz and Budget are the bigger ones, but many new private firms (e.g., Pragocar and Brnocar) have emerged.

## 7. Gasoline

Four basic kinds of gasoline are available: Special (90 octane), Super (96 octane), Diesel, and unleaded, called "Natural". The unleaded gas is usually available only in big cities and on major routes.

## 8. Traffic Rules

Since there are some differences between traffic rules and signs in the United States and Czech Republic, it is suggested to check with an autoclub and get familiar with the rules and signs. The most significant differences include: no right turn on red; no four way stops; the rule of right-of-way - it is strictly enforced at intersections; and zero blood alcohol content. The speed limit is 110 km/hour on highways, 90 km/hour on other roads and the city limit is 60 km/hour unless specified differently.

## CURRENCY

The official Czech currency is the Czech Crown (Česká koruna - Kč). One crown equals 100 hellers (haléř). You can exchange your foreign currency or traveler's checks at almost any bank, the airport, the main train stations, some hotels, and small bank satellites at city centers. Your passport may be required for this transaction. Due to the fact the currency is not fully convertible yet, it is suggested to keep your receipts otherwise you may not be able to change your money back to the hard currency. Do not exchange your money with anybody on the street. Make sure that you are familiar with the exchange rate. As of March 1994 the rate was 29.80 Kč for 1 USD.

You may use major credit cards at some hotels, shops, and restaurants. The credit card sticker will be posted on the door. It may be harder to find a place that will accept a credit card once you leave Prague.

## SHOPPING

Food stores are generally open from 7:00 or 8:00 a.m. to 6:00 p.m. (sometimes until 9:00 p.m.) on weekdays and until noon on Saturdays. Most of the stores are closed on Sundays. Supermarkets are not very common but there are smaller self-service stores. In addition, you will find many small specialty stores, e.g., meat, baked goods, fruit and vegetables, milk products. The quality and quantity of food is good. Fresh fruits and vegetables can be also found at farmers' markets which are held daily in most big cities and on certain days (usually Saturday mornings) in smaller towns.

Other stores, including department stores, are usually open from 8:00 or 9:00 a.m to 6:00, 7:00 or 8:00 p.m. on weekdays with longer hours on Thursdays. They close at noon or 2:00 p.m. on Saturdays and are closed on Sundays.

The Czech Republic is famous for its crystal which is available in department stores and glass specialty stores. Many street vendors sell crystal, but be careful with their pricing. Other items which are a good value include: china, pottery, leather goods, CD's, and books.

## EATING OUT

Do not expect to find a wide variety of restaurants like in the United States. There are very few Chinese, Japanese, or Indian restaurants, especially after you leave Prague. Mexican restaurants are unheard of. On the other hand, good ethnic restaurants can be found throughout the country. Make sure you also visit some of the pubs and breweries. Better restaurants in Prague often require reservations. Very few restaurants have separate smoking and non-smoking sections, but smoking is prohibited during lunch time (11:00 a.m. - 2:00 p.m.).

Lunch is the biggest meal of the day. You may be served soup, a main dish, and a salad which comes with the main dish. The salad dressing is very different, usually just water with lemon or vinegar and sugar and a little salt and pepper. Mixed salads are not very common. You will not be able to find many vegetarian restaurants or salad bars. In a regular restaurant a non-meat meal would be either a sweet dish or an egg and cheese dish.

The proper way to use your utensils is different from the American way. Hold the knife in your right hand (if you are right-handed) and the fork in your left hand throughout the meal. Cut one bite of food at a time. When you are done, put both utensils on the plate next to each other. This is a signal for the waiter to take your plate. If you leave them crossed on the plate, it means that you are not done with your meal yet.

Typical Czech Dishes:
- Roast pork with dumplings and sauerkraut
 (Vepřové maso / vepřová pečeně s knedlíky a se zelím)
- Sirloin of beef with dumplings and creamy vegetable sauce
 (Svíčková pečeně s knedlíky)
- Wiener schnitzel with potatoes or potato salad
 (Řízek s brambory / bramborovým salátem)
- Goulash
 (Guláš)

Tipping is different than in the USA. It is about 5% - 10% and is usually used to round-up the amount. For example:
11.50 Kč → 12 Kč, 22.80 Kč → 24 Kč, 97 Kč → 100 Kč.


**RECREATION**

The ring of mountains surrounding the country provides many excellent opportunities for recreation. Many Czechs own summer cottages or mountain chalets where they spend most of their weekends. Tourists can take advantage of many hotels, hostels, and especially private bed and breakfast places to spend some time in the mountains. The mountains are not very high and are mostly forested. Mountain biking is becoming very popular and many places have bikes available for rent. Skiing is considered a national sport. If you plan to do some skiing you may expect longer lift lines and shorter runs than at the larger U.S. ski resorts. If you stay in the city, you may enjoy a soccer game or play tennis.

## HOLIDAYS

Banks, stores, and offices are closed on official holidays which include:
    January 1 - New Year's Day
    Easter Monday
    May 1 - May Day
    May 8 - End of World War II in Europe (1945)
    July 5 - Day of Cyril and Methodius (863)
    July 6 - Anniversary of the death of Jan Hus (1415)
    October 28 - Day of the foundation of the Czechoslovak
             Republic (1918)
    December 24 - Christmas Eve
    December 25 - First Christmas holiday
    December 26 - Second Christmas holiday

Other observed holidays, but regular working days:
    May 5 - Day of uprising in Prague (1945)
    November 17 - Students' day (1939)

## TIME

The Czech Republic falls into the Central European time zone. Time differences as compared to Prague include:
    London - 1 hour behind Prague
    New York - 6 hours behind Prague
    Los Angeles - 9 hours behind Prague
*Example:*
New York: 10 a.m. - Prague: 4 p.m.

Daylight saving time is used from the end of March through the end of September. Clocks go forward one hour the last Saturday in March and back an hour on the final Saturday of September.

Time of day, days of the week, and months vocabulary can be found in Lesson 5. The first day of the week is Monday. Even though the Czechs use military time, 12 hour form is often given.

## POST OFFICE

The post office is open on weekdays from 8:00 a.m. until 6:00 p.m and on Saturdays from 8:00 a.m. until noon. The main post office in Prague is in Vodičkova Street near Wenceslas Square. Mail boxes are orange and are either mounted on buildings or stand on the streets or sidewalks.

## TELEPHONE

Local calls cost 2 Kč from a pay phone. In Prague, a pay phone can be found at every subway station. Lift the receiver, insert your money, and dial the number. If you need to make an international call, you can dial directly from the pay phone using the country code (the code for USA is 001), however, you will need a lot of coins. It is cheaper to place the call from a post office than to call from your hotel room.

Emergency numbers throughout the country:
Medical: 155
Police:    158
Fire:      150

## REST ROOMS

Rest rooms are labeled as follows:
WC (water closet), OO, Záchody (toilets).
Ladies' Rooms: Ženy or Dámy.
Men's Rooms: Muži or Páni.
Payment for using Ladies' room is usually required in the amount of 1 - 2 Kč.

## ELECTRICITY/APPLIANCES

Appliances operate on 220V AC, 50 Hz. Unless your appliance can be switched to 220V, a converter will be necessary. In either case you will need an adapter, since electrical plugs have a round pin shape.

The TV functions on Pal/Secam system and for that reason standard US TV and video equipment is not compatible.

## CUSTOMS AND COURTESIES

If you are invited to a Czech home for dinner you will want to arrive on time. It is customary to bring a small gift, e.g, flowers, bottle of wine, or chocolate candies. If you receive a gift, you are not obligated to send back a thank you card.

Czechs usually shake hands when they meet. It is still a custom to open the door for a woman and to take her coat. On the other hand, when entering a restaurant the man should enter first.

# Czech Language

The Czech language belongs to the Slavic language group. This family of languages can be geographically divided into three groups:
1. Western: Czech, Slovak, and Polish.
2. Eastern: Russian, Byelorussian, and Ukrainian.
3. Southern: Slovenian, Serbo-Croatian, and Bulgarian.

There are many grammar and vocabulary similarities among the Slavic languages. Czech and Slovak are especially close. A native speaker who knows either of the two languages can easily understand the other one.

The Czech language was created from the preslavic language, believed to be used by slavic tribes from around 2,000 BC through the 7th century AD. Evidence of the Czech language goes back to the 9th century. It was influenced by the Old Slavonic language which was used mainly for religious, literary, and legal matters. Old Slavonic was replaced by Latin in the 11th century. The 12th to 16th centuries can be characterized as a period of evolution of the Czech language. This process was interrupted at the beginning of the 17th century when the German language began to gain its dominant role. Strong nationalistic movement in the first half of the 19th century emphasized the importance of native language. The scientific basis of the language that was introduced in this era was further developed in the second half of the 19th century.

Today, Czech is spoken by about ten million people. The language is fairly uniform throughout Bohemia with some local dialects in the border areas. Moravia has its own dialect. However, the language taught in schools and used by the media (national Czech) is the same in both regions. The main difference between national Czech and colloquial Czech is in the vowel endings of nouns and adjectives.

# Abbreviations

| | |
|---|---|
| acc. | accusative case |
| adj. | adjective |
| adv. | adverb |
| anim. | animate |
| c. | case |
| dat. | dative case |
| dir. | direction |
| f. | feminine |
| gen. | genitive case |
| imp. | imperfective verb |
| imper. | imperative |
| inan. or inanim. | inanimate |
| inst. | instrumental case |
| lit.: | literally |
| loc. | location |
| m. | masculine |
| n. | neuter |
| nom. | nominative case |
| p. | person |
| perf. | perfective verb |
| pers. | person |
| pl. | plural |
| prep. | prepositional case |
| prepos. | preposition |
| pron. | pronoun |
| sbd. | somebody |
| sing. | singular |
| sth. | something |
| voc. | vocative case |
| vs. | versus |

Declension tables:

| | |
|---|---|
| 1. | 1st case, nominative |
| 2. | 2nd case, genitive |
| 3. | 3rd case, dative |
| 4. | 4th case, accusative |
| 5. | 5th case, vocative |
| 6. | 6th case, prepositional |
| 7. | 7th case, instrumental |

Conjugation tables:

| | |
|---|---|
| 1st | 1st person |
| 2nd | 2nd person |
| 3rd | 3rd person |

<u>Note</u>:

In vocabulary the following rules are followed:

1. Nouns given in nominative singular form unless specified differently. With more difficult nouns gender and pattern given.
2. Adjectives usually given in masculine nominative singular form.
3. Pronouns and numerals usually given in nominative form.
4. If verb pair given, the imperfective verb is listed first and the perfective verb is listed second.
5. If preposition introduced, case of the noun that follows is given in parentheses.

# Pronunciation

## 1. Czech Alphabet and Its Basic Sounds

Czech spelling is very phonetic. It is essential to learn the basic sounds and a few pronunciation rules. Once one is familiar with them, it is easy to read and spell almost any Czech text.

| Letter | Approximate Pronunciation |
|--------|---------------------------|
| A | bus |
| B | book |
| C | hits |
| Č | cheese |
| D | door |
| Ď | duty |
| E | egg |
| F | flat |
| G | glad |
| H | hand |
| CH | "kh", not in English, like German "ch" in "ach" |
| I | bill |
| J | boy |
| K | king |
| L | land |
| M | my |
| N | nobody |

| Letter | Approximate Pronunciation |
|--------|---------------------------|
| Ň | canyon |
| O | not |
| P | park |
| Q | "kv" |
| R | rose |
| Ř | "rž" or "rš", not in English |
| S | snake |
| Š | shield |
| T | Tom |
| Ť | tube |
| U | book |
| V | visit |
| W | visit |
| X | "ks" |
| Y | nobody |
| Z | zebra |
| Ž | pleasure |

The Czech alphabet, like the English alphabet consists of vowels and consonants.

## 2. Vowels

Vowels are either short or long. The basic sounds of long vowels are the same as the sounds of short vowels. Long vowels are pronounced for a longer period of time (approximately twice as long as short vowels). In a text the long vowels are always marked with the accent or stress mark - in Czech called "čárka" or "kroužek."

| Short Vowels | Long Vowels |
|---|---|
| a | á (father) |
| e | é |
| i | í (machine) |
| o | ó (orb) |
| u | ú (rule), at the beginning of a word (únos) |
| | ů (rule), in the middle of a word (nůž) |
| y | ý (see) |

Another classification divides vowels into two groups: hard and soft. Softness of the vowel means that there is a little bit of a Czech "j" sound included ("j" plus the basic vowel sound), especially when combined with a hard consonant. For further information refer to paragraph 3.3.

| Hard Vowels | Soft Vowels |
|---|---|
| y/ý | i/í |
| e | ě |

The Czech language does not have a vowel reduction like German or English. The quality of a vowel does not vary with its position in a word. Every syllable must be clearly pronounced.

## 3. Consonants

Based on the "softness" of the sound, consonants can be divided into three groups: hard, soft, and neutral.

| Hard | h | ch | k | r | d | t | n | | |
|------|---|----|---|---|---|---|---|---|---|
| Soft | ž | š | č | ř | c | j | ď | ť | ň |
| Neutral | b | f | l | m | p | s | v | z | |

This classification is important especially for spelling purposes in distinguishing between using "i" and "y" with the above consonants. Hard consonants mostly take on "y", soft consonants mostly take on "i", and neutral consonants can take on either, depending upon the specific word and its spelling rules. For accuracy check the Czech language dictionary.

*Example*:
chyba - říjen - syn - síla

Another classification divides consonants into the two following groups: voiced and voiceless. Most of the consonants exist in pairs, however, some are either voiced or voiceless.

| Voiced | b | d | ď | g | h | v | z | ž | j | m | n | ň | r | ř | | |
|--------|---|---|---|---|---|---|---|---|---|---|---|---|---|---|---|---|
| Voiceless | p | t | ť | k | ch | f | s | š | | | | | | | c | č |

### 3.1 Neutralization of Final Consonants

Voiced consonants that have voiceless pairs become voiceless at the end of a word.
*Example:*

| pair | spelled | pronounced |
|------|---------|------------|
| b → p: | dub | dup |
| d → t: | hrad | hrat |
| ď → ť: | teď | teť |
| g → k: | geolog | geolok |
| h → ch: | sníh | sních |
| v → f: | mrkev | mrkef |
| z → s: | obraz | obras |
| ž → š: | věž | věš |

## 3.2 Assimilation of Consonants

a) Voiced consonants that have voiceless pairs become voiceless if standing in front of a voiceless consonant.

*Example:*

| spelled | | pronounced |
|---------|---|------------|
| včera | → | fčera |
| vstát | → | fstát |
| obchod | → | opchot |

b) Voiceless consonants that have voiced pairs become voiced if standing in front of a voiced consonant.

*Example:*

| spelled | | pronounced |
|---------|---|------------|
| nikdo | → | nigdo |
| kresba | → | krezba |

Note:
This rule does not apply if "v" is the second consonant in the group.
*Example:*
svolat, svařit - pronounced as spelled

c) When there is a group of three consonants together, the third consonant has the influence on the two preceding ones and determines the quality of the sounds (e.g., voiced or voiceless).

*Example:*

| spelled | | pronounced |
|---------|---|------------|
| vzpružit | → | fspružit |

## 3.3 Combination of Hard Consonants and Soft Vowels

Hard consonant followed by a soft vowel is influenced by the softness of the vowel (the Czech "j" sound in addition to the basic vowel sound). The Czech "j" sound is not pronounced separately but is "built-in" in the consonant.
*Example:*
děti: d pronounced like in **duty**, t like in **tube**

## 4. Diphthongs

There are three diphthongs in the Czech language: au, eu, ou. They are created by pronouncing the basic sound of each letter.

## 5. Stress

Each word in the Czech language is stressed. This stress must not be confused with the length of long vowels. The stress is on the first syllable of the word.

## 6. Intonation

The Czech language has two basic intonations: statement and question. The intonation falls down at the end of a statement but rises at the end of a question.

## 7. Prepositions

Prepositions are pronounced together with the following word.

## EXERCISES

1. *Read the following combinations, pay attention to short and long vowels.*
   ma - má, ve - vé, su - sů, že - žé, jo - jó, ni - ní, ty - tý, bu - bů, di - dí, fa - fá, ce - cé, lo - ló, mama - máma - mamá - mámá

2. *Read the following words.*
   máma, táta, les, park, pes, stůl, zima, dům, čaj, pán, syn, ano, ne, doba, žena, já, on, škola, doma, čekat, psát

3. *Read the following words, pay attention to hard and soft vowels.*
   děti, předměty, hadi, hrady, nikdo, nyní, někdo, vidět, deky, nic, něco, vědět, vidět, vyjet, objev, oběd, platit, stěny, děda, ticho,

tykat, kniha, kotě, země, měřit, měnit

**4. Read the following words, pay attention to voiced and voiceless consonants.**
včera, loď, nikdo, sad, včela, na shledanou, někdo, zub, vstát, hoď, podzim, pošta, Václav, konev, dub

**5. Read the following words, pay attention to neutral consonants.**
mít, mýt, viset, vyjet, bít, být, byt, lysý, líbat, pysk, pískat, zima, Ruzyně

**6. Read the following words, pay attention to diphthongs.**
couvat, koukat, vous, auto, automat, pneumatika, sauna

**7. Read the following words.**
pln, srp, trn, vrstva, pletl, klovl, brzo, frkat
peřej, moře, řeč, řada, dveře, pepř, vařit, řeřicha, bořit
ret, rosa, spor, kůra, modrá, rychle, razit, vrazit
chodit, chleba, chovat, chochol, chromý, chvátat, pochyby
hodit, hledat, hlava, pohyby, tuha, hodit, hrozit, mnoho
pracovat, couvat, pec, přece, cedník, cibule, líce

# Lesson 1

### SEZNÁMENÍ

Let.

Letadlo z New Yorku právě odlétá. Dva manželské páry sedí vedle sebe a hovoří.

| | |
|---|---|
| Josef: | Promiňte, paní. Slyším, že mluvíte česky. Letíte také do Prahy? |
| Jana: | Ano. Je to naše první návštěva od té doby, co jsme odešli z České republiky. |
| Eva: | Letíte do České republiky na dovolenou? |
| Václav: | Ne. Já letím na služební cestu a manželka mne doprovází. Dovolte mi, abych nás představil. Jmenuji se Václav Novák a toto je moje manželka Jana. |
| Josef: | Těší mě. Josef Horák a Eva, moje žena. |
| Eva: | Jaké máte plány v České republice? |
| Jana: | Chceme vidět Prahu a jiná známá místa. |
| Václav: | Co jste dělali ve Spojených státech? |
| Josef: | Byli jsme tady na návštěvě. Kde žijete v Americe? |
| Václav: | V New Yorku. A kde žijete vy? |
| Eva: | V Praze. |
| Jana: | Jaké je vaše zaměstnání? |
| Josef: | Eva je učitelka a já jsem lékař. A co děláte vy? |
| Václav: | Jana pracuje v bance a já jsem počítačový inženýr. |
| Jana: | Máte děti? |
| Eva: | Ano, syna a dceru. Chodí do základní školy. Nyní jsou u babičky. Určitě nám přijdou naproti na letiště. V kolik hodin budeme v Praze? |
| Josef: | Ve tři hodiny odpoledne. |

## MEETING PEOPLE/INTRODUCTION

Flight.

The plane is departing New York. Two married couples are sitting next to each other talking.

| | |
|---|---|
| Josef: | Excuse me. I hear you speaking Czech. Are you also flying to Prague? |
| Jana: | Yes. This is our first visit since we left the Czech Republic. |
| Eva: | Are you flying to the Czech Republic on vacation? |
| Václav: | No, I am going there on a business trip and my wife is accompanying me. Let me introduce us. My name is Václav Novák and this is my wife Jana. |
| Josef: | Pleased to meet you. Josef Horák and my wife Eva. |
| Eva: | What are your plans in the Czech Republic? |
| Jana: | We want to see Prague and other familiar places. |
| Václav: | What did you do in the United States? |
| Josef: | We were here visiting. Where do you live in America? |
| Václav: | In New York. And where do you live? |
| Eva: | In Prague. |
| Jana: | What do you do for a living? |
| Josef: | Eva is a teacher and I am a physician. And what do you do? |
| Václav: | Jana works in a bank and I am a computer engineer. |
| Jana: | Do you have children? |
| Eva: | Yes, a son and a daughter. Both are attending elementary school. They are with their grandmother now. Surely, they will meet us at the airport. What time do we arrive in Prague? |
| Josef: | Three o'clock in the afternoon. |

## VOCABULARY

| | |
|---|---|
| Američan/Američanka | American male/ female |
| Amerika | America |
| angličtina | English language |
| ano | yes |
| babička | grandmother |

| | |
|---|---|
| banka | bank |
| bydlet (imp.) | to live, to reside |
| být | to be |
| co | what |
| čas | time (free time) |
| Čech/Češka | Czech male/female |
| čekat | to wait |
| Česká republika | Czech Republic |
| česky | Czech (adv.) |
| český | Czech (adj.) |
| čeština | Czech language |
| dcera | daughter |
| dědeček | grandfather |
| děkovat (imp.) | to thank |
| dělat/udělat | to do |
| dítě/děti | child/children |
| dnes | today |
| doba | period |
| doma (adv.) | at home |
| doprovázet (imp.) | to accompany |
| dovolit (perf.) | to allow |
| dům | house |
| hodina | hour/lesson |
| hovořit (imp.) | to talk |
| chtít (imp.) | to want |
| inženýr | engineer |
| já | I |
| jak | how |
| jeden (m.), jedna (f.), jedno (n.) | one |
| jmenovat se (imp.) | to be called |
| kde | where |
| kdo | who |
| lékař/lékařka | physician male/female |
| lekce (f.) | lesson |
| let | flight |
| letadlo | airplane |
| letiště | airport |
| letět (imp.) | to fly |
| matka | mother |
| manžel/manželka | husband/wife |
| manželský pár | married couple |

| | |
|---|---|
| místo (noun) | place |
| mít (imp.) | to have |
| mluvit/promluvit | to speak |
| muž | man/husband |
| my | we |
| na (prepos., acc./prep.) | on, at |
| náš | our, ours |
| návštěva | visit |
| navštívit | to visit |
| ne | no |
| nyní | now |
| odejít | to leave |
| odlétat (imp.) | to depart (by plane) |
| odpoledne | afternoon |
| on | he |
| ona | she |
| oni | they |
| ono | it |
| otec | father |
| pán | Mr. |
| paní | Mrs. |
| plán | plan |
| počítač | computer (noun) |
| počítačový | computer (adj.) |
| práce (f.) | work |
| pracovat (imp.) | to work |
| Praha | Prague |
| právě | right now |
| prominout | to forgive |
| první | first |
| představovat se/představit se | to introduce oneself |
| přijít naproti | to meet |
| republika | republic |
| s, se (prepos., inst.) | with |
| sedět (imp.) | to sit |
| seznámení | introduction (person to person) |
| služební cesta | business trip |
| slyšet/uslyšet | to hear |
| Spojené státy | the United States |
| Spojené státy americké | the United States of America |
| syn | son |

| škola | school |
| tady | here |
| také | also |
| to | it, that, this |
| učit/naučit | to teach/to learn |
| učitel/učitelka | teacher male/female |
| určitě | surely |
| v, ve (prepos., acc./prep.) | in |
| vedle | next to |
| vidět/uvidět | to see |
| vy | you (pl.) |
| základní | basic |
| základní škola | elementary school |
| zaměstnání | employment/work/job |
| známý | familiar/known |
| žena | wife |
| žít (imp.) | to live |

## EXPRESSIONS

| Dobrý den. | Hello (lit.: Good day.). |
| Dobré ráno. | Good morning. |
| Dobré odpoledne. | Good afternoon. |
| Dobrý večer. | Good evening. |
| Dobrou noc. | Good night. |
| Ahoj. | Hi/Bye. (used only with friends) |
| Na shledanou. | Good-bye. |
| Ano. | Yes. |
| Ne. | No. |
| Děkuji. | Thank you. |
| Prosím. | You are welcome. / Please. / Here you are. |
| Promiňte. | Excuse me. (formal or pl.) |
| Promiň. | Excuse me. (familiar sing.) |
| Jak se jmenujete? | What is your name? (formal or pl.) |
| Jak se jmenuješ? | What is your name? (familiar sing.) |
| Jmenuji se... | My name is... |
| Kde bydlíte? | Where do you live? (formal or pl.) |
| Kde bydlíš? | Where do you live? (familiar sing.) |
| Těší mě. | (I am) Pleased to meet you. |

Těší nás.                    (We are) Pleased to meet you.


## GRAMMAR

### 1. Personal Pronouns

| PERSONAL PRONOUNS | | | | |
|---|---|---|---|---|
| **person** | **singular** | | **plural** | |
| 1st | já | I | my | we |
| 2nd | ty | you | vy | you |
| 3rd | on | he | oni | they |
| | ona | she | ony | they |
| | ono | it | ona | they |

Note:
Please notice two different Czech translations of English "you." *Ty* - the familiar or friendly "you" is used when talking with children, friends, or younger people. *Vy* - the plural or polite/formal "you" is used for addressing older people, superiors, or people we do not know very well.


### 2. Addressing People

Generally, when meeting a new person, one starts by using the polite "you" - vy. There is not a written age limit, but normally by the age of 15 one will start using the polite form. People use the polite/formal form unless both parties decide and agree on the familiar form. If a name is used, one starts with the polite form and uses the expression Mr. (pán), Mrs. (paní), or Miss (slečna) and the last name. First names are used mostly among friends.

## 3. Verbs to Be, to Have

### 3.1 Present Tense of to Be (Být)

| BÝT | | | |
|---|---|---|---|
| já jsem | I am | my jsme | we are |
| ty jsi | you are | vy jste | you are |
| on/ona/ono je | he/she/it is | oni jsou | they are |

Note:
The "j" sound at the beginning of a word is often not pronounced if it is followed by another consonant, e.g., jsem is pronounced "sem".

### 3.2 Present Tense of to Have (Mít)

| MÍT | | | |
|---|---|---|---|
| já mám | I have | my máme | we have |
| ty máš | you have | vy máte | you have |
| on/ona/ono má | he/she/it has | oni mají | they have |

## 4. Negation

The prefix **ne-** is used to make a negative sentence. It is added to the verb it negates.
*Example:*

| | | |
|---|---|---|
| mluvit | → | nemluvit |
| mít | → | nemít |
| jsem | → | nejsem |
| je | → | není (the negative form of je is **není**) |

Czech language is not restricted to one negation in a sentence.
*Example*:
Nikdo není dnes doma.                   Nobody is home today.
(lit.:Nobody is not home today.)

Nikdo nic neví.                           Nobody knows anything.

**EXERCISES**

**1.** *Fill in the right form of the verbs "být" and "mít."*
   1. Kde (být) Petr? 2. Jana (mít) babičku v Praze. 3. My (mít)
dnes školu. 4. Oni (být) na letišti. 5. Ona (být) na návštěvě.
6. Petr a Jana (být) muž a žena. 7. (Mít - 2nd pers. sing.) dnes
čas? 8. Kdo (být) s Petrem doma?

**2.** *Answer the following questions positively and negatively.*
   1. Máš čas? 2. Je Petr doma? 3. Je to dědeček? 4. Jsou Petr a
Jana muž a žena? 5. Máš počítač? 6. Jsi dnes ve škole? 7. Je
to čeština?

**3.** *Translate.*
   1. What is your name? 2. Where do you live? 3. Hi. 4. Good-bye.
5. Good afternoon. 6. Pleased to meet you. 7. My name is Václav
Novák. 8. Excuse me. 9. What do you do for a living?

**4.** *Put the following sentences in a negative form.*
   1. Mluvím česky. 2. Eva je učitelka. 3. Letím na služební cestu.
4. Mám babičku. 5. Ten inženýr se jmenuje Horák. 6. Dcera
hovoří s matkou. 7. Otec a syn jsou lékaři.

**5.** *Conversation.*
   1. Mluvíte česky?
   2. Letíte také do Prahy?
   3. Letíte do České republiky na dovolenou?
   4. Jaké máte plány v Praze?
   5. Kde žijete ve Spojených státech?
   6. Jaké je vaše zaměstnání?
   7. V kolik hodin budeme v Praze?

# Lesson 2

## PASOVÁ A CELNÍ KONTROLA

Přílet.

| | |
|---|---|
| Josef: | Václave, vaše zavazadla si můžete vyzvednout zde. Pasová a celní kontrola je tam. |
| Václav: | Děkuji. |
| Pasový úředník: | Dobré odpoledne. Vaše pasy, prosím. Mluvíte česky? |
| Václav: | Ano. Narodili jsme se tady. |
| Pasový úředník: | Jak dlouho budete v České republice? |
| Václav: | Tři týdny. |
| Pasový úředník: | Děkuji. Prosím, pokračujte k celní kontrole. |
| Celník: | Dobré odpoledne. Máte něco k proclení? |
| Jana: | Ne. Vezeme jen malé dárky. |
| Celník: | Otevřete, prosím, tento kufr. |
| Jana: | Jistě. |
| Celník: | Všechno je v pořádku. Děkuji. Přeji vám pěkný pobyt. |
| Jana, Václav: | Na shledanou. |

## PASSPORT CONTROL AND CUSTOMS

Arrival.

| | |
|---|---|
| Josef: | Václav, you can pick up your luggage here. Passport control and customs are over there. |
| Václav: | Thank you. |
| Passport Officer: | Good afternoon. Your passports, please. Do you speak Czech? |
| Václav: | Yes. We were born here. |
| Passport Officer: | How long will you be in the Czech Republic? |
| Václav: | Three weeks. |

| Passport Officer: | Thank you. Please, proceed to customs. |
| Customs Officer: | Good afternoon. Do you have anything to declare? |
| Jana: | No. We are bringing only small presents. |
| Customs Officer: | Open this suitcase, please. |
| Jana: | Of course. |
| Customs Officer: | Everything is in order. Thank you. Have a nice stay. |
| Jana, Václav: | Good-bye. |

## VOCABULARY

bez (prepos., gen.) — without
celní kontrola — customs
celník — custom officer
číst (imp.) — to read
dárek — gift/present
do (prepos., gen.) — to, into, till
druhý — second
dva (m.), dvě (f., n.) — two
hrad — castle
chodit/jít — to go (by foot)/to attend
jet/jezdit — to go (by transportation)
jistě — of course
kniha — book
knihovna — library
kolej (f.) — dormitory
kost (f.) — bone
kufr — suitcase
kuře — chicken
malý — small
město — city/town
moci — can, to be able to
moře — sea
most — bridge
naproti (prepos., dat.) — opposite to, across from
narodit se — to be born
nebo — or
něco — something
někdo — somebody/someone

| | |
|---|---|
| noc (f.) | night |
| o (prepos., prep.) | about |
| otevírat/otevřít | to open |
| park | park |
| pas | passport |
| pasová kontrola | passport control |
| pec (f.) | oven |
| pěkný | nice |
| pobyt | stay |
| pokračovat | to proceed, to continue |
| pole | field |
| pořádek | order |
| pro (prepos., acc.) | for |
| proclení | declaration |
| přát/popřát | to wish |
| před (prepos., acc./inst.) | in front of, before |
| předseda (m.) | chairman |
| přílet | arrival (by plane) |
| ráno | morning |
| růže (f.) | rose |
| řidič | driver |
| slovo | word |
| soudce (m.) | judge |
| stavení | building |
| stroj | machine |
| student/studentka | student male/female |
| stůl | table/desk |
| tam | over there/there |
| tento | this |
| týden | week |
| u (prepos., gen.) | by |
| věda | science |
| velký | big/large |
| vézt/odvézt | to carry, to transport (by vehicle) |
| všechno (pron.) | all |
| vyzvednout | to pick-up, to get |
| z, ze (prepos., gen.) | from |
| za (prepos., acc./inst.) | behind, in back of |
| zámek | chateaux/lock |
| zavazadlo | luggage |
| zde, tady, tu | here |

**GRAMMAR**

## 1. Article

The Czech language does not have definite or indefinite articles. Translation into English depends upon the context.

*Example:*

Čtu knihu.                I am reading a book.
Přečetl jsem tu knihu.    I have read the book.

## 2. Declension

In Czech, nouns, adjectives, pronouns, and numerals are declined. This means their endings are changed based upon the function of the word within the sentence.

Note:
The ending is the part of the word that is changed through declension (or conjugation of verbs).

## 3. Nouns

### 3.1 Gender of Nouns

The Czech language has three genders: masculine, feminine, and neuter. Czech gender is not a logical category (as in English), but a grammatical category. The gender of a Czech noun is determined by the ending, not by the meaning of the word. However, expressions referring to male beings are usually masculine and expressions referring to female beings are usually feminine. Animals, plants, and things can be masculine, feminine, or neuter. Masculine nouns are further divided into animate and inanimate groups.

*Example*:

žena(f.),  muž (m.),  park (m.), škola (f.), město (n.), kuře (n.)

#### 3.1.1 Noun Endings

a)     Masculine Nouns:
       Most masculine nouns end with a consonant. There are four

basic groups of masculine nouns:
1. Masculine Animate Hard (nouns ending with a hard or neutral consonant): pattern **pán**.
2. Masculine Animate Soft (nouns ending with a soft consonant): pattern **muž**.
3. Masculine Inanimate Hard (nouns ending with a hard or neutral consonant): pattern **hrad**.
4. Masculine Inanimate Soft (nouns ending with a soft consonant): pattern **stroj**.

b)   Feminine Nouns:
Most feminine nouns end with -a. There are four groups of feminine nouns:
1. Nouns ending with an -a: pattern **žena**.
2. Nouns ending with an -e: pattern **růže**.
3. Nouns ending with a soft consonant: usually pattern **kolej**.
4. Nouns ending with a hard or neutral consonant: usually pattern **kost**.

c)   Neuter Nouns:
Most neuter nouns end with an -o. There are four groups of neuter nouns:
1. Nouns ending with an -o: pattern **město**.
2. Nouns ending with an -e: pattern **moře**.
3. Nouns ending with an -e and mostly expressing baby animals: pattern **kuře**.
4. Nouns ending with an -í: pattern **stavení**.

Note:
1. Nouns which end with a consonant or an -e and are feminine are marked in the vocabulary.
2. Be aware of exceptions to the above classification. For accuracy check the Czech language dictionary.

### 3.2 Declension of Nouns

The Czech language has seven cases:
1. Nominative: Expresses the subject or predicate of the sentence. (His *mother* called. She is his *mother*.)
2. Genitive: Expresses possession. (The mother of your *friend*.)

3. <u>Dative</u>: Expresses the indirect object. (The mother of your friend gave *me* a book.)
4. <u>Accusative</u>: Expresses the direct object. (The mother of your friend gave me a *book*.)
5. <u>Vocative</u>: Expresses direct address. (*Mother, look!*)
6. <u>Prepositional</u>: Expresses the object of a preposition - e.g., location or meaning "about". (The mother of your friend gave me a book about *Prague*.)
7. <u>Instrumental</u>: Expresses the agent or the instrument of an action. (The letter was written by the *mother* of your friend. The letter was written by a *pen*.) The instrumental case also expresses mutual participation. (I live with my *friend*.)

<u>Note</u>:
Some more difficult verbs and prepositions associated with a particular case are marked in the vocabulary.

### 3.2.1  Declension of Patterns

Each group of nouns belongs to a specific declension and pattern that must be memorized in order to know how to decline the particular word.

| DECLENSION OF MASCULINE NOUNS | | | | |
|---|---|---|---|---|
| **singular** | | | | |
| case | animate | | inanimate | |
| 1. | **pán** | **muž** | **hrad/les** | **stroj** |
| 2. | pána | muže | hradu/lesa | stroje |
| 3. | pánovi/-u | mužovi/-i | hradu | stroji |
| 4. | pána | muže | hrad | stroj |
| 5. | pane | muži | hrade | stroji |
| 6. | pánovi/-u | mužovi/-i | hradě/lese/ zámku | stroji |
| 7. | pánem | mužem | hradem | strojem |

| DECLENSION OF MASCULINE NOUNS | | | |
|---|---|---|---|
| **plural** | | | |
| 1. | **páni/-ové** | **muži/-ové** | **hrady** | **stroje** |
| 2. | pánů | mužů | hradů | strojů |
| 3. | pánům | mužům | hradům | strojům |
| 4. | pány | muže | hrady | stroje |
| 5. | páni | muži | hrady | stroje |
| 6. | pánech | mužích | hradech/ lesích/ zámcích | strojích |
| 7. | pány | muži | hrady | stroji |

Note:
1. There are two more patterns for masculine animate nouns: **předseda, soudce.** Words belonging to them are used less frequently.
2. Some nouns undergo various stem changes as they are being declined.
   *Example*:
   - otec (nom. sing.) - otce (gen. sing.) - otče (voc. sing.)
   - stůl (nom. sing.) - stolu (gen. sing.)
   - zámek (nom. sing.) - zámku (gen. sing.)
   The above examples show not only consonant changes, but a "fleeting" vowel rule as well. This rule applies only to some nouns and means that the stem vowel is dropped through the declension, except of nominative (animate and inanimate) and accusative (inanimate) cases, e.g., zámek.
3. Hard inanimate nouns can have two or three different endings in the case. The proper ending used depends upon the specific word.
   *Example*:
   - prepositional singular: -e/-ě/-u: lese/hradě/zámku.
4. Some nouns have an option in using one of the two available endings.
   *Example*:
   - nominative plural: -i/-ové: páni/pánové.

| case | singular | | | |
|------|------|------|------|------|
| DECLENSION OF FEMININE NOUNS | | | | |
| 1. | žena | růže | kolej | kost |
| 2. | ženy | růže | koleje | kosti |
| 3. | ženě | růži | koleji | kosti |
| 4. | ženu | růži | kolej | kost |
| 5. | ženo | růže | kolej | kost |
| 6. | ženě | růži | koleji | kosti |
| 7. | ženou | růží | kolejí | kostí |

| case | plural | | | |
|------|------|------|------|------|
| 1. | ženy | růže/ulice | koleje | kosti |
| 2. | žen | růží/ulic | kolejí | kostí |
| 3. | ženám | růžím | kolejím | kostem |
| 4. | ženy | růže | koleje | kosti |
| 5. | ženy | růže | koleje | kosti |
| 6. | ženách | růžích | kolejích | kostech |
| 7. | ženami | růžemi | kolejemi | kostmi |

Note:
In the dative and prepositional cases *b, f, m, p, v* plus -e change to *bě, fě, mě, pě, vě; d, n, r, t* plus -e change to dě, ně, ře, tě; and *g, h, ch, k* plus -e change to *ze, ze, še, ce.*
*Example:*
kniha - knize, věda - vědě

| DECLENSION OF NEUTER NOUNS | | | |
|---|---|---|---|
| **case** | singular | | |
| 1. | **město** | **moře** | **kuře** | **stavení** |
| 2. | města | moře | kuřete | stavení |
| 3. | městu | moři | kuřeti | stavení |
| 4. | město | moře | kuře | stavení |
| 5. | město | moře | kuře | stavení |
| 6. | městu/ě | moři | kuřeti | stavení |
| 7. | městem | mořem | kuřetem | stavením |
| **case** | plural | | |
| 1. | **města** | **moře** | **kuřata** | **stavení** |
| 2. | měst | moří | kuřat | stavení |
| 3. | městům | mořím | kuřatům | stavením |
| 4. | města | moře | kuřata | stavení |
| 5. | města | moře | kuřata | stavení |
| 6. | městech | mořích | kuřatech | staveních |
| 7. | městy | moři | kuřaty | staveními |

## EXERCISES

1. *Note the following nouns' gender and assign each noun to a declension category.*

| | | |
|---|---|---|
| kontrola | slovo | odpoledne |
| republika | student | most |
| dárek | stůl | ráno |
| kniha | zavazadlo | noc (f.) |
| kufr | čas | židle (f.) |
| pas | dítě | řidič |
| pořádek | lekce | místo |
| proclení | manžel | letadlo |

| | | |
|---|---|---|
| počítač | seznámení | škola |
| pole | lékař | pec (f.) |

**2. Decline the nouns in the following sentences.**
1. Hana je ve (škola - prep.). 2. Kdy máš (čeština - acc.)? 3. Kolej je naproti (most - gen.). 4. Jana má (růže - acc.). 5. Letadlo letí do (Praha - gen). 6. Student čte (kniha - acc.) u (stůl - gen.). 7. Knihovna je za (most - inst.). 8. On má (slovo - acc.).

**3. Translate.**
1. I am an American. 2. I live in Texas. 3. My name is ---. 4. I have a book. 5. The school is behind the bridge. 6. Your passports, please. 7. Do you speak Czech? 8. I was born there.

**4. Conversation.**
1. Jsi Američan/Američanka?
2. Jak se jmenuješ?
3. Kde bydlíš?
4. Jak dlouho budete v České republice?
5. Máte něco k proclení?

# Lesson 3

## MÍSTNÍ DOPRAVA

Taxi.

Horákovi se setkali s dětmi a babičkou na letišti.

| | |
|---|---|
| Dcera: | Maminko, jaký byl let? |
| Eva: | Dobrý. Seznámili jsme se s velmi sympatickými lidmi. |
| Josef: | Pojďme domů. Kde je stanoviště taxi? |
| Syn: | Tam. |
| Řidič: | Dobré odpoledne. Kam chcete jet? |
| Josef: | Plzeňská ulice 25 (dvacet pět). Víte, kde to je? |
| Řidič: | Ano. Myslím, že budete potřebovat dvě auta. Máte příliš mnoho zavazadel. |
| Josef: | To nevadí. Manželka pojede s dětmi. Evo, sejdeme se doma. |
| Řidič: | Máme štěstí. Není velký provoz. |
| Josef: | Zastavte, prosím. Tady bydlíme. Kolik to stojí? |
| Řidič: | Taxametr ukazuje 87 (osmdesát sedm) korun. |
| Josef: | Tady je 90 (devadesát) korun, to je v pořádku, nechte si drobné. Můžete mi dát účet, prosím? |
| Řidič: | Samozřejmě. |
| Josef: | Děkuji. Na shledanou. |
| Řidič: | Na shledanou. |

## LOCAL TRANSPORTATION

Taxi.

The Horáks are met by their children and grandmother at the airport.

Daughter:    Mom, how was the flight?

| Eva: | Good. We met some very nice people. |
| Josef: | Let's go home. Where is a taxi stand? |
| Son: | Over there. |
| Taxi Driver: | Good afternoon. Where do you want to go? |
| Josef: | Pilsen Street 25. Do you know where that is? |
| Taxi Driver: | Yes. I think that you will need two cars. You have too much luggage. |
| Josef: | It does not matter. My wife will go with the children. Eva, we will meet at home. |
| Taxi Driver: | We are lucky. The traffic is not bad. |
| Josef: | Stop, please. We live here. How much is it? |
| Taxi Driver: | The meter shows 87 crowns (Kč). |
| Josef: | Here is 90 crowns, it's O.K., keep the change. Can you give me a receipt, please? |
| Taxi Driver: | Of course. |
| Josef: | Thank you. Good-bye. |
| Taxi Driver: | Good-bye. |

## VOCABULARY

| | |
|---|---|
| anglicky | English (adv.) |
| anglický | English (adj.) |
| auto | car |
| brát (imp.) | to take |
| člověk/lidé | person/people |
| dávat/dát | to give |
| dobrý | good (adj.) |
| dobře | good (adv.) |
| domů | home (adv.,dir.) |
| dopis | letter |
| doprava | transportation/traffic |
| drobné (peníze) | change |
| hala | hall |
| hodně | a lot/plenty |
| jaký | what kind/what |
| jazyk | language/ tongue |
| k, ke (prepos., dat.) | to, toward |
| kam | where (direction) |
| kino | movie theater |
| koruna | crown (Czech currency) |

| | |
|---|---|
| krýt (imp.) | to cover |
| který | which one |
| kupovat/koupit | to buy |
| lidé, lidi | people |
| mazat (imp.) | to spread |
| mezi (prepos., acc./inst.) | between/among |
| minout (imp.) | to pass/to miss |
| místní | local |
| mnoho | many/plenty |
| myslet (imp.) | to think |
| myslet na (acc.) | to think about |
| nosit/nést | to carry |
| od (prepos., gen.) | from |
| péci/upéci | to bake |
| platit/zaplatit za (acc.) | to pay for |
| pod (prepos., acc./inst.) | under/underneath |
| potřebovat (imp.) | to need |
| prosit/poprosit | to ask for |
| provoz | traffic |
| psát/napsat | to write |
| rozumět (imp.) | to understand |
| říkat/říci | to tell/to say |
| samozřejmě | of course |
| sázet (imp.) | to plant |
| setkávat se/setkat se | to meet sbd. |
| seznamovat se/seznámit se | to be introduced to sbd./to meet sbd. |
| scházet se/sejít se | to meet w/sbd. |
| stanoviště | stop (noun) |
| studovat (imp.) | to study |
| sympatický | nice, likable |
| štěstí | luck |
| taxametr | meter |
| taxi, taxík | taxi |
| tisknout/natisknout | to print |
| trpět (imp.) | to suffer |
| třetí | third |
| tři | three |
| účet | bill/receipt |
| ukazovat/ukázat | to show |
| ulice | street |
| umřít | to die |

| vadit (imp.) | to matter/to hamper |
| vědět (imp.) | to know sth. |
| velmi | very |
| začínat/začnout | to begin, to start |
| zastavovat/zastavit | to stop |
| znát/poznat | to know sbd. or sth./to recognize |
| že | that |

**EXPRESSIONS**

| To nevadí. | Never mind. It doesn't matter. |
| Hodně štěstí. | Good luck. |
| Máme štěstí. | We are lucky. |

## GRAMMAR

### 1. Verbs

#### 1.1 Present Tense - Conjugation of Verbs

Verbs are divided into five classes according to the ending of the 3rd person singular as follows:

| CONJUGATION OF VERBS - PRESENT TENSE | | | | |
|---|---|---|---|---|
| **FIRST CLASS** | | | | |
| **person** | **pattern** | | | |
| | **nést** | **brát** | **mazat** | **péci** | **umřít** |
| já | nesu | beru | mažu/-i | peču | umřu |
| ty | neseš | bereš | mažeš | pečeš | umřeš |
| on | nese | bere | maže | peče | umře |
| my | neseme | bereme | mažeme | pečeme | umřeme |
| vy | nesete | berete | mažete | pečete | umřete |
| oni | nesou | berou | mažou/-í | pečou | umřou |

Note:
Only some verbs with -ž, -š, -č in the stem can use both endings in
the 1st person singular and 3rd person plural. The rest of the verbs
must use the -u and -ou endings.

| CONJUGATION OF VERBS - PRESENT TENSE | | | | |
|---|---|---|---|---|
| **SECOND CLASS** | | | **THIRD CLASS** | |
| **person** | **pattern** | | **pattern** | |
| | tisknout | minout | začnout | krýt | kupovat |
| já | tisknu | minu | začnu | kryji | kupuji |
| ty | tiskneš | mineš | začneš | kryješ | kupuješ |
| on | tiskne | mine | začne | kryje | kupuje |
| my | tiskneme | mineme | začneme | kryjeme | kupujeme |
| vy | tisknete | minete | začnete | kryjete | kupujete |
| oni | tisknou | minou | začnou | kryjí | kupují |

| CONJUGATION OF VERBS - PRESENT TENSE | | | |
|---|---|---|---|
| **FOURTH CLASS** | | | **FIFTH CLASS** |
| **person** | **pattern** | | **pattern** |
| | prosit | trpět | sázet | dělat |
| já | prosím | trpím | sázím | dělám |
| ty | prosíš | trpíš | sázíš | děláš |
| on | prosí | trpí | sází | dělá |
| my | prosíme | trpíme | sázíme | děláme |
| vy | prosíte | trpíte | sázíte | děláte |
| oni | prosí | trpí | sázejí | dělají |

1.1.1 Conjugation of Some Frequently Used Verbs

|     | psát    | chtít  | číst  | vědět |
|-----|---------|--------|-------|-------|
| já  | píšu/-i | chci   | čtu   | vím   |
| ty  | píšeš   | chceš  | čteš  | víš   |
| on  | píše    | chce   | čte   | ví    |
| my  | píšeme  | chceme | čteme | víme  |
| vy  | píšete  | chcete | čtete | víte  |
| oni | píšou/-í| chtějí | čtou  | vědí  |

### 1.2 Perfective and Imperfective Verbs

Most of the Czech verbs exist in two forms: perfective and imperfective.

Perfective verbs express an action with respect to a single point in time such as beginning of an action, completion or termination of an action. They express single, total, complete event and/or its result (e.g., I finished my work.). The perfective verbs are very often created from imperfective verbs by adding a prefix.

Imperfective verbs express continuous, repetitive, habitual action with no reference to the length of time it takes or with no reference to the specific point of its beginning or completion (e.g., I am finishing my work.).

*Example:*
číst (imp.) - přečíst (perf.)
Čtu každý večer.                     I read every evening.
Včera večer jsem četl.               I was reading yesterday evening.
Včera večer jsem přečetl             I read (finished reading)
novou knihu.                         a new book  yesterday evening.

Note:
In the vocabulary, the imperfective verb is marked (imp.); if verb pair given, the imperfective verb is listed first and the perfective

verb is listed second.
*Example*: udělat/dělat.

## 1.3 Past Tense

There is only one form of the past tense, so called compound past tense. It is a combination of an auxiliary verb and the verb that carries the meaning. The past tense is formed by dropping the -t of the infinitive, adding the **-l** (m.), **-la** (f.), **-lo** (n.) endings. Also, if the exposed vowel is long, it will be shortened (dát - dal). The present tense of the verb "být" in the first and second person is added. The plural endings are as follows: masculine animate **-li**, masculine inanimate and feminine **-ly**, and neuter **-la**.

| PAST TENSE ||
| --- | --- |
| **person** | **verb** |
| já | jsem dělal/**-a/-o** |
| ty | jsi dělal/**-a/-o** |
| on/ona/ono | dělal/**-a/-o** |
| my | jsme dělal**i**/**-y/-a** |
| vy | jste dělal**i**/**-y/-a** |
| oni/ony/ona | dělal**i**/**-y/-a** |

Note:
1. If the infinitive ends with **-nout**, the past tense has two different forms based upon the pattern the verb belongs to:
   a) the -ou is shortened to -u (minout - minul).
   b) the -nout drops entirely (poslechnout - poslechl).
2. The past tense ending always depends upon the gender of the subject of the sentence, not on the sex of the person talking.
3. Notice that when the personal pronoun is present, the position of the auxiliary verb changes.
   *Example*:
   dělal jsem vs. já jsem dělal

1.3.1  Past Tense of the Verbs "Být", "Mít", "Jít", and "Chtít"

| present tense | být | mít | jít | chtít |
|---|---|---|---|---|
| past tense | byl | měl | šel/šla/šlo | chtěl |

### 1.4  Future Tense

There are two forms of the future tense in Czech: compound and simple. The form to be used depends upon the aspect of the verb carrying the meaning.

Compound future tense is used for imperfective verbs. It is created by using the future form of the auxiliary verb "být" (to be) and the infinitive form of the verb carrying the meaning.

Simple future tense is used for perfective verbs. These verbs do not have a present tense, therefore their "present" conjugation actually expresses future.

| FUTURE TENSE | | | |
|---|---|---|---|
| person | verb "být" | compound | simple |
| já | budu | budu slyšet | uslyším |
| ty | budeš | budeš slyšet | uslyšíš |
| on/ona/ono | bude | bude slyšet | uslyší |
| my | budeme | budeme slyšet | uslyšíme |
| vy | budete | budete slyšet | uslyšíte |
| oni | budou | budou slyšet | uslyší |

Note:
1. The negative form of imperfective verbs is formed by adding the **ne-** prefix to the future tense of the verb "být."
   *Example*:
   nebudu slyšet
2. The negative form of perfective verbs is formed by adding the

negative prefix **ne-** to the meaning verb.
*Example*:
neuslyším

## EXERCISES

1. *Classify the following verbs and give their 3rd person singular and 3rd person plural forms.*

| | | | |
|---|---|---|---|
| tisknout | dávat | dát | kupovat |
| mluvit | slyšet | vidět | nosit |
| pracovat | minout | rozumět | studovat |
| bydlet | letět | číst | jmenovat se |

2. *Put the following verbs into all three tenses (present/past/future).*
1. Hana (mluvit) anglicky. 2. Jana (psát) dopis. 3. My (jet) do Prahy. 4. (Bydlet-2nd pers. sing.) ve Spojených státech? 5. Petr a Jan (pracovat) ve škole. 6. Jaké (znát-2nd pers. pl.) jazyky? 7. Já a Petr (jít) do kina.

3. *Translate.*
1. I live in the United States. 2. Where is a taxi stand? 3. Peter, we will meet across from the movie theater. 4. Stop, please! 5. Good luck. 6. It does not matter.

4. *Conversation.*
1. Mluvíš česky?
2. Studuješ češtinu nebo angličtinu?
3. Kde pracuješ?
4. Co je to?
5. Co děláš ve škole?

# Lesson 4

## UBYTOVÁNÍ

V hotelu.

Novákovi právě přijeli do hotelu Ambassador.

Václav:     Dobré odpoledne. Jmenuji se Václav Novák. Objednal jsem si telefonicky pokoj pro dva.
Recepční:   Ano, pane Novák. Vyplňte, prosím, tento formulář. Děkuji. Tady jsou klíče. Číslo vašeho pokoje je 312 (tři sta dvanáct). Je to ve třetím poschodí. Výtah je vpravo vedle schodiště. Vaše zavazadla budou v pokoji za okamžik.
Václav:     Kde můžeme parkovat?
Recepční:   V podzemním parkovišti hotelu.
Jana:       Můžete mi říci, kde dostaneme snídani?
Recepční:   Restaurace je v prvním patře. Snídaně se podává od 7 (sedmi) do 10 (deseti) hodin ráno. Snídani si také můžete objednat na pokoj.
Václav:     Je snídaně zahrnutá v ceně?
Recepční:   Ne, není.
Jana:       Můžete mi říci, jaké jiné služby poskytuje váš hotel?
Recepční:   V přízemí je směnárna, obchod se suvenýry a holičství a kadeřnictví. Tělocvična je v suterénu.
Jana:       Děkuji.
Recepční:   Když budete něco potřebovat, zatelefonujte na recepci.

## ACCOMMODATIONS

In the Hotel.

The Nováks have just arrived at the Ambassador Hotel.

| | |
|---|---|
| Václav: | Good afternoon. My name is Václav Novák. I reserved a room for two by phone. |
| Clerk: | Yes, Mr. Novák. Fill out this form, please. Thank you. Here are the keys. Your room number is 312. It is on the third floor. The elevator is on your right next to the stairway. Your luggage will be in your room in a moment. |
| Václav: | Where can we park? |
| Clerk: | In the hotel's underground parking lot. |
| Jana: | Can you tell me where we get breakfast? |
| Clerk: | The restaurant is on the first floor. Breakfast is served from 7 to 10 a.m. You can also order breakfast in your room. |
| Václav: | Is breakfast included in the price? |
| Clerk: | No, it is not. |
| Jana: | Can you also tell me what other services your hotel offers? |
| Clerk: | There is a money exchange, souvenir shop, barber shop, and a hair dresser on the first floor. There is an exercise room in the basement. |
| Jana: | Thank you. |
| Clerk: | If you need anything, call the front desk. |

## VOCABULARY

| | |
|---|---|
| ale | but |
| cena | price |
| číslo | number |
| čtvrtý | fourth |
| čtyři | four |
| déšť | rain |
| dovolená | vacation |
| formulář | form |
| hledat (imp.) | to look for sbd./sth. |
| hned | immediately, right away |
| holičství | barber shop |
| hotel | hotel |
| hudba | music |
| jen/jenom | only |
| jiný | other/different |

| | |
|---|---|
| kabát | coat |
| kadeřnictví | hair dresser/beauty shop |
| Karlova universita | Charles University |
| klíč | key |
| konec | end |
| květina | flower |
| líbit se (imp.) | to like |
| mladý | young |
| obal | cover |
| obchod | store |
| objednávat/objednat | to order |
| obloha | sky |
| obraz | picture/painting |
| okamžik | moment |
| parkovat/zaparkovat | to park |
| parkoviště (n.) | parking lot |
| patro | floor (e.g., 3rd floor) |
| pero | pen |
| počasí | weather |
| podávat (imp.) | to serve |
| podzemní | underground (adj.) |
| pokoj | room |
| poschodí | floor (e.g., 3rd floor) |
| poskytovat/poskytnout | to offer |
| přednáška | lecture |
| přijet | to come (by transportation) |
| přízemí | first floor |
| rád (short adj.) | to like |
| recepce | front desk |
| recepční | front desk clerk |
| restaurace (f.) | restaurant |
| sešit | notebook |
| schodiště (n.) | stairway |
| slunce (n.) | sun |
| služba | service |
| směnárna | money exchange |
| snídaně (f.) | breakfast |
| sníh | snow |
| starý | old |
| strom | tree |
| sukně (f.) | skirt |

| | |
|---|---|
| suterén | basement |
| suvenýr | souvenir |
| svetr | sweater |
| tamten | that (one) |
| telefon | telephone |
| telefonicky | by phone |
| tělocvična | exercise room |
| ten (m.)/ta (f.)/to (n.) | that |
| tenhle | this (one) |
| tráva | grass |
| ubytování | accommodations, lodging |
| universita or univerzita | university |
| váš | your, yours |
| volat/zavolat | to call/to telephone |
| vpravo | on the right |
| výlet | trip |
| vyplnit | to fill in/out |
| výtah | elevator |
| začátek | beginning |
| zahrnutý | included |
| zatelefonovat | to call, to telephone |
| zkušenost (f., kost) | experience |
| židle (f.) | chair |

| **barvy** | **colors** |
|---|---|
| bílá | white |
| černá | black |
| červená | red |
| fialová | purple |
| hnědá | brown |
| modrá | blue |
| oranžová | orange |
| růžová | pink |
| stříbrná | silver |
| šedá | grey |
| zelená | green |
| zlatá | gold |
| žlutá | yellow |

| **roční období** | **seasons** |
|---|---|
| *noun/adj.* | |

| jaro/jarní | spring |
| léto/letní | summer |
| podzim/podzimní | fall |
| zima/zimní | winter |

## GRAMMAR

### 1. Adjectives

The Czech language has three categories of adjectives: hard, soft, and possessive (see Lesson 9). The adjective must always agree with the noun it modifies in terms of gender, number, and case. Adjectives are declined similarly to nouns. The declensions vary by gender.

### 1.1 Hard Adjectives

This category includes all adjectives whose nominative singular form ends with the following hard vowels:
-ý: masculine
-á: feminine
-é: neuter

| DECLENSION OF HARD ADJECTIVES | | | | |
|---|---|---|---|---|
| | **singular** | | | |
| case | masculine animate | masculine inanimate | feminine | neuter |
| 1.&5. | mladý | mladý | mladá | mladé |
| 2. | mladého | mladého | mladé | mladého |
| 3. | mladému | mladému | mladé | mladému |
| 4. | mladého | mladý | mladou | mladé |
| 6. | mladém | mladém | mladé | mladém |
| 7. | mladým | mladým | mladou | mladým |

| DECLENSION OF HARD ADJECTIVES | | | |
|---|---|---|---|
| **plural** | | | |
| 1.&5. | mladí | mladé | mladé | mladá |
| 2. | mladých | mladých | mladých | mladých |
| 3. | mladým | mladým | mladým | mladým |
| 4. | mladé | mladé | mladé | mladá |
| 6. | mladých | mladých | mladých | mladých |
| 7. | mladými | mladými | mladými | mladými |

*Example*:
Mladý muž, mladá žena, mladé dítě.

Note:
"Jaký" and "který" are declined as pattern *mladý*.

## 1.2  Soft Adjectives

This category includes all adjectives whose nominative singular form
ends with the soft vowel  **-í** .
Note:
The ending is the same for all genders.

| DECLENSION OF SOFT ADJECTIVES | | | | |
|---|---|---|---|---|
| **singular** | | | | |
| case | masculine animate | masculine inanimate | feminine | neuter |
| 1.&5. | jarní | jarní | jarní | jarní |
| 2. | jarního | jarního | jarní | jarního |
| 3. | jarnímu | jarnímu | jarní | jarnímu |
| 4. | jarního | jarní | jarní | jarní |
| 6. | jarním | jarním | jarní | jarním |
| 7. | jarním | jarním | jarní | jarním |

| DECLENSION OF SOFT ADJECTIVES | | | |
|---|---|---|---|
| **plural** | | | |
| 1.&5. | jarní | jarní | jarní | jarní |
| 2. | jarních | jarních | jarních | jarních |
| 3. | jarním | jarním | jarním | jarním |
| 4. | jarní | jarní | jarní | jarní |
| 6. | jarních | jarních | jarních | jarních |
| 7. | jarními | jarními | jarními | jarními |

*Example*:
Jarní les, jarní květina, jarní počasí.

## 2. Demonstrative Pronouns

Similar to nouns and adjectives, pronouns are also declined. The demonstrative pronoun must agree with the noun it modifies in terms of gender, number, and case. The English translation is "this" or "that."

| DECLENSION OF DEMONSTRATIVE PRONOUNS | | | | |
|---|---|---|---|---|
| **singular** | | | | |
| case | masculine animate | masculine inanimate | feminine | neuter |
| 1.&5. | ten | ten | ta | to |
| 2. | toho | toho | té | toho |
| 3. | tomu | tomu | té | tomu |
| 4. | toho | ten | tu | to |
| 6. | tom | tom | té | tom |
| 7. | tím | tím | tou | tím |

| | | | |
|---|---|---|---|
| **DECLENSION OF DEMONSTRATIVE PRONOUNS** | | | |
| **plural** | | | |
| 1.&5. | ti | ty | ty | ta |
| 2. | těch | těch | těch | těch |
| 3. | těm | těm | těm | těm |
| 4. | ty | ty | ty | ta |
| 6. | těch | těch | těch | těch |
| 7. | těmi | těmi | těmi | těmi |

**2.1 Demonstrative Pronouns "Tento", "Tenhle", "Tamten"**

The suffixes **-to, -hle** and the prefix **tam-** narrow the meaning of the basic demonstrative pronouns. "Tato" or "tahle kniha" means this book right here. "Tamta kniha" means the book over there or the book we saw in the past.

**3. Words Expressing an Indefinite Quantity**

Adverbs expressing an indefinite quantity (e.g., kolik/how much, několik/several, tolik/so much, mnoho/much, trochu/a little bit, and málo/few) put the dependent noun in a genitive case but the verb is in the 3rd person singular.
*Example*:
Kolik amerických studentů (gen.) studovalo na Karlově universitě?   How many American students studied at Charles University?
O češtině je málo knih (gen.).   There are few books about the Czech language.

**4. Czech Expression for "To Like"**

a) mít rád   to like sbd. or sth.
b) rád + verb carrying meaning   to like to

*Example*:

| | |
|---|---|
| Mám rád tu knihu. | I like that book. |
| Rád čtu tu knihu. | I like to read that book. |
| Mám rád Petra. | I like Peter. |
| Mám tě rád. | I like (love) you. |

Note:
1. If understood from the context, the personal pronoun may be left out: (Já) mám rád tu knihu.
2. The form of the word "rád" depends upon the gender and number of the speaker: rád (m.), ráda (f.), rádo (n.), rádi/rády/ráda (pl.).
3. The form of the verb "mít" also depends upon the gender and number of the speaker.

| | |
|---|---|
| c) líbit se | to like sbd. or sth. |

*Example*:

| | |
|---|---|
| Ten obraz se mi líbí. | I like the painting. (lit.: The painting is pleasing to me.) |
| Petr se mi líbí. | I like Peter. |
| Já se líbím Petrovi. | Peter likes me. |

Note:
The English subject is in the dative case in the Czech sentence, and the direct object becomes the subject of the Czech sentence.

**EXERCISES**

**1. *Decline the following adjectives.***
1. Matka ráda nosí (červená - acc., sing.) sukni. 2. V knihovně mají (zelená - acc., pl.) židle. 3. Václav hledá ten (modrý - acc., sing.) svetr. 4. Půjdeš v tom (černý - prep., sing.) kabátě? 5. Co je to na tom (žlutý - prep., sing.) stole? 6. Jakou barvu má ta kniha? (Fialová - acc., sing.) nebo (bílá - acc., sing)? 7.

Potřebujeme ten sešit, ale bez toho (zlatý - gen., sing.) obalu. 8. Milan a Eva jdou k té (žlutá - dat., sing.) škole. 9. Máš s sebou to (stříbrné - acc., sing.) pero. 10. S (modrá - inst., sing.) barvou mám (dobrá - acc., pl.) zkušenosti. 11. Mám rád (jarní - acc., sing.) čas. 12. Milan je na (letní - prep., sing.) dovolené. 13. S (podzimní - inst., sing.) počasím je konec. 14. Karel rád jezdí na (zimní - acc., pl.) výlety. 15. Krásné (beautiful) jsou (zlatá - nom., pl.) a (červená - nom., pl.) barvy v (podzimní - prep., sing.) slunci.

**2. Answer the following questions.**
1. Jakou máš ráda barvu? 2. Jakou barvu má tvůj svetr? 3. Jsi Američan/ka? 4. V kterém státě bydlíš? 5. Co budeš dnes dělat? 6. Čteš ráda knihy nebo posloucháš hudbu?

**3. Insert the correct demonstrative pronoun.**
1. Mám ráda ... (acc., sing.) knihu. 2. Kde je ... (nom., sing.) učitel? 3. Kam jdeš s ... (inst., sing.) Češkou? 4. To je ... (nom., sing.) barva. ... (acc., sing.) barvu mám rád. 5. Viděla jsem Pavla v ... (prep., sing.) novém svetru. 6. Letěli jsme v ... (prep., sing.) letadle. 7. Půjdu tam bez ... (gen., sing.) inženýra. 8. Jana mluvila o ... (prep., sing.) staré ženě. 9. Viděla jsem Petra v ... (prep., sing.) tělocvičně. 10. Kdy začne ... (nom., sing.) přednáška?

**4. Match the right colors and give proper adjective endings.**
Tráva je        modrý
Obloha je       červený
Slunce je       zelený
Kuře je         bílý
Strom je        žlutý
Sukně je        zelený
Sníh je         zlatý

**5. Conversation.**
1. Kam právě Novákovi přijeli?
2. Jaký pokoj si Václav objednal?
3. V kterém poschodí je pokoj číslo 312?
4. Kde mohou Novákovi parkovat?

5. Kde se podává snídaně?
6. V kterém hotelu bydlí Václav a Jana?
7. Co je v přízemí hotelu?

# Lesson 5

PTANÍ SE NA CESTU

Cestou na poštu.

| | |
|---|---|
| Jana: | Promiňte, prosím, vás, můžete mi říci, kde je zde pošta? |
| Chodec: | Pošta není daleko. Můžete tam jít pěšky. Jděte rovně po této ulici až na první křižovatku. Na křižovatce zahněte doleva. Tam uvidíte banku. U banky zahněte doprava. Jděte přibližně 150 (sto padesát) metrů až k obchodnímu domu Kotva. Pošta je hned vedle. |
| Jana: | Je možné jet k poště městskou dopravou? |
| Chodec: | Ano. Můžete jet tramvají číslo 6 (šest). První zastávka je "Museum". Druhá zastávka je obchodní dům "Kotva". Tam musíte vystoupit a budete přímo před poštou. |
| Jana: | Děkuji, na shledanou. |
| Chodec: | Prosím, na shledanou. |

Na poště.

| | |
|---|---|
| Václav: | Dobré odpoledne. Chtěli bychom poslat tyto dopisy do Spojených států. Kolik to stojí letecky? |
| Úředník: | Cena je podle váhy. Je to 9 (devět) korun. |
| Václav: | Kdy budou dopisy v New Yorku? |
| Úředník: | Přibližně za týden. |
| Václav: | Děkuji, na shledanou. |
| Úředník: | Prosím, na shledanou. |

**ASKING FOR DIRECTIONS**

On the Way to the Post Office.

| Jana: | Excuse me, please, can you tell me where there is a post office here? |
| Pedestrian: | The post office is not very far. You can walk there. Go straight on this street to the first intersection. At the intersection turn left. There you will see a bank. At the bank turn right. Go about 150 meters to the department store "Kotva". The post office is right next to it. |
| Jana: | Is it possible to go to the post office by public transportation? |
| Pedestrian: | Yes. You can take streetcar number 6. The first stop is "Museum". The second stop is the department store "Kotva". There you have to get off and you will be right in front of the post office. |
| Jana: | Thank you, good-bye. |
| Pedestrian: | You are welcome, good-bye. |

### At the Post Office

| Václav: | Good afternoon. We would like to send these letters to the United States. How much is it by air mail? |
| Clerk: | It depends upon the weight. It is 9 crowns. |
| Václav: | When will the letters be in New York? |
| Clerk: | Approximately one week. |
| Václav: | Thank you, good-bye. |
| Clerk: | You are welcome, good-bye. |

## VOCABULARY

| | |
|---|---|
| adresa | address |
| autobus | bus |
| až | till, until |
| blízko | near (adv.) |
| blízký | near (adj.) |
| březen | March |
| cesta | way/trip |
| cizí | foreign |
| červen | June |
| červenec | July |
| čtvrtek | Thursday |

| | |
|---|---|
| daleko | far (adv.) |
| daleký | far (adj.) |
| datum (n., město) | date |
| den | day |
| dívka/holka | girl |
| doleva | to the left |
| doprava | to the right |
| dostávat/dostat | to get |
| duben | April |
| haléř | heller : Czech unit of money, 100 hellers = 1 crown |
| hlavní | main |
| hned | immediately/right away |
| chlapec/hoch/kluk | boy |
| chodec | pedestrian |
| kdy | when |
| kolik | how much |
| koruna (Kč) | crown: Czech unit of money |
| křižovatka | intersection |
| květen | May |
| leden | January |
| letecky | by plane/air mail |
| letos | this year |
| listopad | November |
| literatura | literature |
| loni | last year |
| měsíc | month/moon |
| městský | city (adj.), meaning public, local |
| metr | meter |
| milión | million |
| minuta | minute |
| moderní | modern |
| možná | maybe |
| muset | must |
| museum or muzeum (n., město) | museum |
| nalevo | on the left |
| napravo | on the right |
| národní | national |
| nastupovat/nastoupit | to get on |
| neděle | Sunday |
| nula | zero |

| | |
|---|---|
| nový | new |
| obchodní | department (adj.) |
| obchodní dům | department store |
| odpověď | answer |
| odpovídat/odpovědět | to answer |
| opakovat (imp.) | to repeat |
| pamatovat si (imp.) | to remember |
| pátek | Friday |
| pátý | fifth |
| peníze (pl. stroj) | money |
| pěšky | on foot (adv.) |
| pět | five |
| podle | along/according to |
| pondělí | Monday |
| posílat/poslat | to send |
| pošta | post office |
| prosinec | December |
| přibližně | approximately |
| přímo | directly |
| příští | next |
| příští rok | next year |
| ptát se/zeptat se | to ask |
| rok | year |
| rovně | straight |
| rozdíl | difference |
| říjen | October |
| slovník | dictionary |
| sobota | Saturday |
| srpen | August |
| stát | to cost/to stand |
| sto | hundred |
| století | century |
| středa | Wednesday |
| tisíc | thousand |
| tramvaj (f.) | streetcar |
| třída | class/classroom |
| únor | February |
| úředník/úřednice | clerk male/female |
| úterý | Tuesday |
| váha | weight/scale |
| včera | yesterday (adv.) |

| veřejný | public (adj.) |
|---|---|
| vlak | train |
| vystupovat/vystoupit | to get off |
| zahýbat/zahnout | to turn |
| zajímat se o (acc.) | to be interested in |
| září | September |
| zastávka | stop (noun) |
| zítra | tomorrow (adv.) |

**EXPRESSIONS**

| Kolik to stojí? | How much is it? |
|---|---|
| Kolik je hodin? | What time is it? |
| V kolik hodin? | At what time? |
| Co je dnes za den? | What day is it today? |
| Kolikátého je dnes? | What is the date today? |
| Jakou máš adresu? | What is your address? |

**GRAMMAR**

**1. Cardinal Numerals**

| 0 | nula | | | | |
|---|---|---|---|---|---|
| 1 | jeden/jedna/jedno | 11 | jedenáct | 30 | třicet |
| 2 | dva/dvě/dvě | 12 | dvanáct | 40 | čtyřicet |
| 3 | tři | 13 | třináct | 50 | padesát |
| 4 | čtyři | 14 | čtrnáct | 60 | šedesát |
| 5 | pět | 15 | patnáct | 70 | sedmdesát |
| 6 | šest | 16 | šestnáct | 80 | osmdesát |
| 7 | sedm | 17 | sedmnáct | 90 | devadesát |
| 8 | osm | 18 | osmnáct | | |
| 9 | devět | 19 | devatenáct | | |
| 10 | deset | 20 | dvacet | | |

| 100 | (jedno) sto (n.) | 600 | šest set |
|---|---|---|---|
| 200 | dvě stě | 700 | sedm set |
| 300 | tři sta | 800 | osm set |
| 400 | čtyři sta | 900 | devět set |
| 500 | pět set | | |

| | |
|---|---|
| 1 000 | (jeden) tisíc (m.) |
| 1 000 000 | (jeden) milión (m.) |

Note:
Combined numbers, 21, 45 etc. are created the same way as in English:

| | |
|---|---|
| 23 | dvacet tři |
| 45 | čtyřicet pět |
| 103 | sto tři |
| 1 256 | tisíc dvě stě padesát šest |

**1.1 Gender and Declension of Cardinal Numerals**

The numbers 1 and 2 use different forms depending upon the gender of the noun they modify.
*Example*:
jeden muž, jedna žena, jedno dítě
dva muži, dvě ženy, dvě děti

The number 1 is declined the same as ten/ta/to.

| DECLENSION OF NUMERAL 1 | | | | |
|---|---|---|---|---|
| case | masculine animate | masculine inanimate | feminine | neuter |
| 1.&5. | jeden | jeden | jedna | jedno |
| 2. | jednoho | jednoho | jedné | jednoho |
| 3. | jednomu | jednomu | jedné | jednomu |
| 4. | jednoho | jeden | jednu | jedno |
| 6. | jednom | jednom | jedné | jednom |
| 7. | jedním | jedním | jednou | jedním |

| DECLENSION OF NUMERALS 2, 3, 4 | | | |
|---|---|---|---|
| case | 2 | 3 | 4 |
| 1. | dva/dvě/dvě | tři | čtyři |
| 2. | dvou | tří | čtyř |
| 3. | dvěma | třem | čtyřem |
| 4. | dva/dvě/dvě | tři | čtyři |
| 6. | dvou | třech | čtyřech |
| 7. | dvěma | třemi | čtyřmi |

Numbers from 5 to 19 as well as 20, 30,..., 90 end with **-i** in all cases except for nominative, accusative, and vocative.
*Example*:
With 15 students.   S patnácti studenty.

The number 100 (sto) is declined as pattern *město*.

The number 1 000 (tisíc) is declined as pattern *stroj*.

The number 1 000 000 (milión) is declined as pattern *hrad*.

Note:
1. The number 1 takes a singular verb, numbers 2, 3, and 4 take a plural verb, and the rest of the numerals (5 and higher) take a singular verb.
*Example*:
**Je** jedna hodina.                    It is one o'clock.
**Jsou** čtyři hodiny                    It is four o'clock.
**Je** deset hodin.                      It is ten o'clock.
2. The case of the noun following the numeral is determined as follows:
   1:              noun is in nominative singular: 1 hodina
   2,3,4:          noun is in nominative plural: 2 hodiny
   5 and higher:   noun is in genitive plural: 5 hodin
3. The same rules as in Note 1 & 2 apply to combined numbers, e.g., 21, 32.

4. The Czech comma represents the English decimal point.
*Example:*
Czech: 2 350,65                    English: 2,350.65

## 2. Time

| | |
|---|---|
| Kolik je hodin? | What time is it? |
| Je jedna hodina. | It is one o'clock. |
| Jsou tři hodiny. | It is three o'clock. |
| Je šest hodin. | It is six o'clock. |
| Je šest (hodin) třicet (minut). | It is six (o'clock) thirty (minutes). |
| Jsou čtyři (hodiny) čtyřicet pět (minut). | It is four (o'clock) forty-five (minutes). |
| V kolik hodin? | At what time? |
| V jedenáct hodin. | At eleven o'clock. |

Note:
The Czechs often use military time, e.g., 11 p.m. is 23 hours.

## 3. Days of the Week

The Czech week starts with Monday and names of days are not capitalized.

| | |
|---|---|
| pondělí | Monday |
| úterý | Tuesday |
| středa | Wednesday |
| čtvrtek | Thursday |
| pátek | Friday |
| sobota | Saturday |
| neděle | Sunday |

Czech language uses the preposition "v/ve" in place of the English preposition "on." The noun that follows the preposition is in the accusative case.
Example:
v pondělí - on Monday

Note:
Preposition "ve" is used with the following days: středa (Wednesday)
and čtvrtek (Thursday).

## 4. Months of the Year

Again, the names of the months are not capitalized.

| leden | January | červenec | July |
|-------|---------|----------|------|
| únor | February | srpen | August |
| březen | March | září | September |
| duben | April | říjen | October |
| květen | May | listopad | November |
| červen | June | prosinec | December |

## 5. Date

The Czech language uses a different format to record dates. It starts
with the day, then month and year.
*Example*:
May 1, 1993 is 1.5.1993 or 1. května 1993.

The date is spoken in the following form: day and month in genitive
and year in nominative.
*Example*:
Dnes je prvního května 1993. Today is May 1st 1993.
Note:
Ordinal numerals are used to express the date. For further
information refer to Lesson 8, paragraph 3.

The year can be pronounced in two different ways:
a) tisíc devět set devadesát tři
b) devatenáct set devadesát tři

## 6. Money

The Czech currency is the Czech crown (Koruna česká - Kč).
1 koruna = 100 haléřů (hellers)

| | |
|---|---|
| Kolik stojí ta kniha? | How much is that book? |
| Ta kniha stojí dvacet pět korun | That book is twenty- |
| a deset haléřů. | five crowns and ten hellers. |

## EXERCISES

**1.** *Answer the following questions using the full date when appropriate.*
1. Kolikátého je dnes? 2. Kdy jste se narodil? 3. Od kdy jste v Praze? 4. Kolikátého bude zítra? 5. Kdy začíná škola? 6. Co je dnes? 7. Jaký je to rok?

**2.** *What time is it?*
5:30, 10:22, 16:45, 19:33, 6:50, 9:15, 12:00, 23:20, 8:40, 11:55.

**3. Answer the following questions.**
1. Kolik stojí ta červená sukně? (425,60 Kč) 2. Kolik stojí ten modrý kabát? (2893,70 Kč) 3. V kolik hodin budeš doma? 4. V kolik hodin jdeš do práce? 5. Kolik stál ten bílý stůl? (7503,50 Kč)

**4. Read the following phone numbers.**

| 21 873 | 56 22 412 | 011 42 2 9971 456 |
|---|---|---|
| 74 025 | 0306 27 642 | 24 17 67 |

**5.** *Decline the adjective and/or noun in the parentheses.*
1. Hledala jsi Janu před (druhá hodina - inst.)? 2. Kolik studentů bylo v (pátá třída - prep.)? 3. Opakujeme s (Petr - inst.) nová slova. 4. S (Američani - inst.) mluvíme anglicky. 5. Tady máte literaturu o (cizí jazyky - prep.).

**6.** *Conversation.*
1. Jak se jmenuje ta dívka, vedle které jsi seděla u stolu?
2. Pamatuješ si, kde je ta knihovna?
3. Jaké knihy tě zajímají?
4. Jde Jana na poštu pěšky nebo tam jede?
5. Kde je pošta?
6. Jakou tramvají musí Jana jet?
7. Kde musí vystoupit?
8. Kolik to stojí poslat dopisy letecky do New Yorku?

# Lesson 6

## NA VEČEŘI

V restauraci.

| | |
|---|---|
| Václav: | Dobrý večer. Zamluvili jsme si stůl na jméno Novák. |
| Číšník: | Dobrý večer. Prosím, pojďte za mnou. Bude vám tento stůl vyhovovat? |
| Václav: | Bohužel ne. Je příliš blízko k hudbě. |
| Číšník: | A tento stůl v rohu by vám vyhovoval? |
| Václav: | Ano, děkuji. |
| Číšník: | Co si dáte k pití? |
| Eva: | Skleničku bílého vína, prosím. |
| Jana: | Pro mne pomerančový džus. |
| Josef: | Já si dám pivo - Plzeňský Prazdroj. |
| Václav: | Pro mne také. Už dlouho jsem neměl dobré české pivo. |
| Jana: | Co říkáte, můžeme si připít na tykání? |
| Eva a Josef: | To je dobrý nápad. Připijme si na to. |
| Václav: | Na zdraví ! |
| Číšník: | Máte vybráno? |
| Jana: | Ano, já bych chtěla svíčkovou pečeni s knedlíky. |
| Eva: | Já si dám řízek s bramborovým salátem. |
| Václav: | Já bych chtěl vepřové se zelím a knedlíkem. |
| Josef: | Já si dám guláš. |

Rozhovor při jídle.

| | |
|---|---|
| Josef: | Jak se vám líbí Praha? |
| Jana: | Velmi! Praha se hodně změnila. Některá místa nemůžeme téměř poznat. |
| Václav: | Raději chodíme pěšky. Je obtížné najít místo na parkování a provoz je příliš velký. |
| Eva: | My používáme hodně metro. Je to rychlé a pohodlné. |

| Číšník: | Jak vám chutnalo? Byli jste spokojeni? |
|---|---|
| Václav: | Ano, bylo to výborné. |
| Jana: | Už dlouho jsem nejedla něco tak dobrého. |
| Josef: | Moc jsme si pochutnali. |
| Číšník: | Budete si přát ještě něco jiného? Kávu nebo zákusek? |
| Václav: | Ne, děkujeme. Zaplatíme. Přineste nám účet, prosím. |
| Číšník: | Jistě, okamžik. |

Vrchní přináší účet. Václav platí a nechává spropitné.

## HAVING DINNER OUT

### In a Restaurant.

| Václav: | Good evening. We have reserved a table under the name Novák. |
|---|---|
| Waiter: | Good evening. Follow me, please. Will this table suit you? |
| Václav: | Unfortunately not. It is too close to the music. |
| Waiter: | Would this table in the corner suit you? |
| Václav: | Yes, thank you. |
| Waiter: | What would you like to drink? (lit.: What will you get to drink?) |
| Eva: | A glass of white wine, please. |
| Jana: | Orange juice for me. |
| Josef: | I will have a beer - Pilsner Urquell. |
| Václav: | For me, too. I have not had a good Czech beer for a long time. |
| Jana: | What do you say, can we toast to using our first names? |
| Eva, Josef: | It is a good idea. Let's toast to that. |
| Václav: | Cheers! |
| Waiter: | Are you ready to order? (lit.: Have you selected?) |
| Jana: | Yes, I would like the sirloin of beef with dumplings. |
| Eva: | I will have the Wiener schnitzel with potato salad. |
| Václav: | I would like the pork roast with sauerkraut and dumplings. |
| Josef: | I will have the goulash. |

Conversation during Dinner.

| | |
|---|---|
| Josef: | How do you like Prague? |
| Jana: | Very much! Prague has changed a lot. We can hardly recognize some places. |
| Václav: | We prefer to walk. It is hard to find a place to park and the traffic is pretty bad. |
| Eva: | We use the subway a lot. It is fast and comfortable. |
| Waiter: | How was everything? (lit.: How did it taste to you?) Were you satisfied? |
| Václav: | Yes, it was delicious. |
| Jana: | I have not eaten anything this good for a long time. |
| Josef: | We enjoyed it very much. |
| Waiter: | Would you like anything else? (lit.: Will you wish anything else?) Coffee or dessert? |
| Václav: | No, thank you. We would like the bill, please. (lit.: Bring us the bill, please.) |
| Waiter: | Sure, just a minute. |

Head waiter brings the bill. Václav pays and leaves a tip.


## VOCABULARY

| | |
|---|---|
| brambora | potato |
| bramborový salát | potato salad |
| bratr | brother |
| čaj | tea |
| číšník/servírka | waiter/waitress |
| dávat si/dát si | to have (in terms of food) |
| džus | juice |
| guláš | goulash |
| hlávkový salát | lettuce |
| hlavní jídlo | main dish |
| hospoda | pub/brewery |
| houska/rohlík | roll |
| hovězí (maso) | beef (meat) |
| chleba | bread |
| chutnat/ochutnat | to taste |
| jablko | apple |

| jeho | his/its |
|---|---|
| její | her, hers |
| jejich | their, theirs |
| jídlo | food |
| jíst/najíst | to eat |
| káva | coffee |
| kavárna | coffee house |
| knedlík | dumpling |
| kyselý | sour |
| litovat (imp.) | to be sorry |
| lžíce (f.) | spoon |
| máslo | butter |
| maso | meat |
| metro | subway |
| míchaný | mixed |
| mléko | milk |
| moc | a lot |
| můj | my, mine |
| nacházet/najít | to find |
| (najdu-1st pers. sing.) | |
| nápad | idea |
| nápoj | drink |
| nechávat/nechat | to leave sth. |
| někde | somewhere |
| někdy | sometime |
| některý | some |
| nějak | somehow |
| nějaký | some kind of |
| nic | nothing |
| nijak | in no way |
| nikde | nowhere |
| nikdo | nobody |
| nikdy | never |
| nůž | knife |
| oběd | lunch |
| obědvat | to eat lunch |
| obtížný | difficult |
| okurka | cucumber |
| ovoce | fruit |
| parkování | parking |
| pepř | pepper |

| | |
|---|---|
| pít (imp.) | to drink |
| pití | drink |
| pivo | beer |
| Plzeňský Prazdroj | Pilsner Urquell |
| pohodlný | comfortable/lazy |
| pochutnat si | to enjoy (meal) |
| polévka | soup |
| pomeranč | orange |
| pomerančový džus | orange juice |
| používat (imp.) | to use |
| poznávat/poznat | to recognize |
| předkrm | appetizer |
| přijít | to come (on foot) |
| příliš | too much |
| přinést | to bring |
| připíjet/připít | to toast |
| raději | rather |
| roh | corner |
| rychlý | fast |
| rýže | rice |
| řízek | (Wiener) schnitzel |
| salát | salad |
| sestra | sister |
| sklenička | glass |
| sladký | sweet |
| snídat | to eat breakfast |
| spokojený | satisfied |
| spropitné | tip |
| sůl | salt |
| svačina | snack |
| svíčková pečeně | sirloin of beef |
| šestý | sixth |
| špatný | bad |
| talíř | plate |
| téměř/skoro | almost |
| tvůj | your, yours |
| tykání | using the familiar form "ty" (and first name) |
| užívat/používat | to use |
| vařit/uvařit | to cook |
| večeře | dinner |

| | |
|---|---|
| večeřet | to eat dinner |
| vepřové (maso) | pork (meat) |
| vidlička | fork |
| vinárna | wine cellar |
| víno | wine |
| voda | water |
| vrchní | head waiter |
| vybírat si/vybrat si | to choose/to select |
| výborný | delicious/excellent |
| vyhovovat/vyhovět | to satisfy/to suit/to accommodate |
| zákusek | dessert |
| zamlouvat/zamluvit | to make a reservation, to reserve |
| zelenina | vegetable |
| zelí | sauerkraut |
| změnit se | to change |
| žádný | none |

## EXPRESSIONS

| | |
|---|---|
| Bohužel ne. | Unfortunately not./Sorry. |
| Na zdraví! | Cheers!/ To your health! |
| Dobrou chuť! | Bon appetite! |
| Všechno je v pořádku. | Everything is all right. |
| Moc mi to chutnalo. | I enjoyed it very much. |
| Bylo to výborné. | It was delicious. |

## GRAMMAR

### 1. Declension of Personal Pronouns

| DECLENSION OF PERSONAL PRONOUNS | | | | | | | | |
|---|---|---|---|---|---|---|---|---|
| 1.&5. | já | ty | on | ona | ono | my | vy | oni |
| 2. | mě/ mne | tebe/ tě | jeho/ ho/jej | jí | jeho/ ho/jej | nás | vás | jich |
| 3. | mně/ mi | tobě/ ti | jemu/ mu | jí | jemu/ mu | nám | vám | jim |
| 4. | mě/ mne | tebe/ tě | jeho/ ho/jej | ji | je/ho/ jej | nás | vás | je |
| 6. | mně | tobě | něm | ní | něm | nás | vás | nich |
| 7. | mnou | tebou | jím | jí | jím | námi | vámi | jimi |

Note:
1. Some pronouns can have two or three forms for one case.
2. If the pronoun of the 3rd person (on, ona, ono, oni etc.) is used with a preposition, then **j-** in the beginning of the word is changed into **n-** and **-e-** is changed into **-ě-**.

*Example:*
Ta knížka patří jemu.  The book belongs to him.
Půjdu k němu.  I will go to him.

## 2. Reflexive Pronoun

The reflexive pronoun refers back to the subject of the sentence.

| REFLEXIVE PRONOUN | |
| --- | --- |
| 1. & 5. | - |
| 2. | sebe |
| 3. | sobě/si |
| 4. | sebe/se |
| 6. | sobě |
| 7. | sebou |

*Example*:
Máš tu knihu s sebou?      Do you have the book with you?
O sobě nic neřekl.          He didn't say anything about himself.


## 3. Reflexive Verbs

Reflexive verbs are verbs that are accompanied by the reflexive pronoun se/si.

Some verbs exist only in reflexive form and the reflexive pronoun does not carry any meaning.
*Example:*
Ptát se.      To ask.
Smát se.      To laugh.
Bát se.       To be afraid.

Other verbs exist in two forms, reflexive and non-reflexive. In that case, the reflexive pronoun can carry a specific meaning such as:
a)  Passivity
    *Example:*
    To se neříká.      It is not said./One does not say that.

b)  Reciprocity
    *Example:*

# 92 *Lesson 6*

Známe se.      We know each other.
Píšeme si.     We write to each other.

c) Reference to the subject of the sentence
   *Example:*
   Koupím si knihu.     I will buy a book for me/myself.
   Ona si to udělá.     She will do it for herself.

Note:
1. The conjugation of a reflexive verb is the same as for a non-reflexive verb.
2. Past tense of 2nd pers. sing. is contracted.
   *Example:*
   Udělal sis. (= udělal jsi si)
3. The reflexive pronoun is placed after the first accented word of the sentence.
   *Example:*
   Kdo si píše?
   Ona si to udělá.
   Jak se jmenuješ?

## 4. Possessive Pronouns

| POSSESSIVE PRONOUNS | | | | |
|---|---|---|---|---|
| **person** | **singular** | | **plural** | |
| 1st | můj (m.)<br>moje (f., n.) | my, mine | náš (m.)<br>naše (f., n.) | our, ours |
| 2nd | tvůj (m.)<br>tvoje (f., n.) | your, yours | váš (m.)<br>vaše (f., n.) | your, yours |
| 3rd | jeho | his | jejich | their, theirs |
| | její | hers | | |
| | jeho | its | | |

Note:
Possessive pronouns must agree with the nouns they modify in terms of gender, number, and case.
*Example:*
můj otec (my father), moje matka (my mother), moje pero (my pen)

## 4.1 Declension of Possessive Pronouns

| DECLENSION OF POSSESSIVE PRONOUNS | | | | | | | |
|---|---|---|---|---|---|---|---|
| **singular** | | | | | | | |
| case | m. inan. | m. anim. | f. | n. | m. inan. | m. anim. | f. | n. |
| 1.&5. | můj | můj | má/ moje | mé/ moje | náš | náš | naše | naše |
| 2. | mého | mého | mé | mého | našeho | našeho | naší | našeho |
| 3. | mému | mému | mé | mému | našemu | našemu | naší | našemu |
| 4. | můj | mého | mou/ moji | mé/ moje | náš | našeho | naši | naše |
| 6. | mém | mém | mé | mém | našem | našem | naší | našem |
| 7. | mým | mým | mou | mým | naším | naším | naší | naším |
| **plural** | | | | | | | |
| 1.&5. | mé/ moje | mí/ moji | mé/ moje | má/ moje | naše | naši | naše | naše |
| 2. | mých | mých | mých | mých | našich | našich | našich | našich |
| 3. | mým | mým | mým | mým | našim | našim | našim | našim |
| 4. | mé/ moje | mé/ moje | mé/ moje | má/ moje | naše | naše | naše | naše |
| 6. | mých | mých | mých | mých | našich | našich | našich | našich |
| 7. | mými | mými | mými | mými | našimi | našimi | našimi | našimi |

## DECLENSION OF POSSESSIVE PRONOUNS

### singular

| case | m. inan. | m. anim. | f. | n. | m. inan. | m. anim. | f. | n. |
|------|----------|----------|----|----|----------|----------|----|----|
| 1.&5. | tvůj | tvůj | tvá/ tvoje | tvé/ tvoje | váš | váš | vaše | vaše |
| 2. | tvého | tvého | tvé | tvého | vašeho | vašeho | vaší | vašeho |
| 3. | tvému | tvému | tvé | tvému | vašemu | vašemu | vaší | vašemu |
| 4. | tvůj | tvého | tvou/ tvoji | tvé/ tvoje | váš | vašeho | vaši | vaše |
| 6. | tvém | tvém | tvé | tvém | vašem | vašem | vaší | vašem |
| 7. | tvým | tvým | tvou | tvým | vaším | vaším | vaší | vaším |

### plural

| case | | | | | | | | |
|------|----------|----------|----|----|----------|----------|----|----|
| 1.&5. | tvé/ tvoje | tví/ tvoji | tvé/ tvoje | tvá/ tvoje | vaše | vaši | vaše | vaše |
| 2. | tvých | tvých | tvých | tvých | vašich | vašich | vašich | vašich |
| 3. | tvým | tvým | tvým | tvým | vašim | vašim | vašim | vašim |
| 4. | tvé/ tvoje | tvé/ tvoje | tvé/ tvoje | tvá/ tvoje | vaše | vaše | vaše | vaše |
| 6. | tvých | tvých | tvých | tvých | vašich | vašich | vašich | vašich |
| 7. | tvými | tvými | tvými | tvými | vašimi | vašimi | vašimi | vašimi |

## DECLENSION OF POSSESSIVE PRONOUNS

| case | singular m. inan. | m. anim. | f. | n. | plural m. inan. | m. anim. | f. | n. |
|---|---|---|---|---|---|---|---|---|
| 1.&5. | její | její | její | její | její | její | její | její |
| 2. | jejího | jejího | její | jejího | jejích | jejích | jejích | jejích |
| 3. | jejímu | jejímu | její | jejímu | jejím | jejím | jejím | jejím |
| 4. | její | jejího | její | její | její | její | její | její |
| 6. | jejím | jejím | její | jejím | jejích | jejích | jejích | jejích |
| 7. | jejím | jejím | její | jejím | jejími | jejími | jejími | jejími |

Note:
1. *Tvůj* is declined the same way as *můj*.
2. *Váš* is declined the same way as *náš*.
3. *Jeho* and *jejich* are not declined.
4. *Její* is declined as a soft adjective (pattern *jarní*).
5. Pronoun *moje*: singular genitive, prepositional, and instrumental cases have also long forms *mojí*. Those forms were used in colloquial Czech. However, because of their frequent usage they are becoming part of the literary language.

## 5. Reflexive Possessive Pronoun

The reflexive possessive pronoun - *svůj* is declined as the 1st person singular - *můj*. It can be translated as any possessive pronoun (my, your, etc.).

## 6. Pronouns Who,What

The pronoun *kdo* (who) is masculine animate singular and the pronoun *co* (what) is neuter singular. They are declined as follows:

| DECLENSION OF PRONOUNS "KDO, CO" | | |
|---|---|---|
| 1. | kdo | co |
| 2. | koho | čeho |
| 3. | komu | čemu |
| 4. | koho | co |
| 6. | kom | čem |
| 7. | kým | čím |

These pronouns are also used for indication of a declension associated with a preposition or verb.

*Example*:
ke komu čemu, pro koho co, o kom o čem, or zajímat se o koho co, rozumět komu čemu.

### 7. Indefinite and Negative Prefixes "Ně-", "Ni-"

The prefix *ně-*, when used with interrogative words, forms an indefinite pronoun/adjective/adverb. The prefix *ni-*, when used with interrogative words, forms a negative pronoun/adjective/adverb.

| co/what | něco/something | nic/nothing |
|---|---|---|
| kdo/who | někdo/somebody/someone | nikdo/nobody/no one |
| kde/where | někde/somewhere | nikde/nowhere |
| kdy/when | někdy/sometime | nikdy/never |
| jaký/what kind | nějaký/some kind of | žádný/none |
| jak/how | nějak/somehow | nijak/in no way |
| který/which, that | některý/some | |

Note:
As mentioned in Lesson 1, the Czech language is not restricted to one negation. If a negative pronoun is used, the verb is used in a

negative form as well.
*Example:*
Já nemám nic.             lit.: I do not have nothing.
Nikdo nemá nic.           lit.: Nobody does not have nothing.


## EXERCISES

**1. Replace singular personal pronouns with plural personal pronouns and vice versa.**
1. Jana šla se mnou (inst.) do kina. 2. Viděli jsme ho (acc.) ve škole. 3. Včera o nich (prep.) mluvili. 4. Ji (acc.) to nezajímá. 5. Byl tam bez nás (gen.). 6. Zítra půjdu s tebou (inst.) do knihovny. 7. Rozumím ti (dat.). 8. Jemu (dat.) to chutná. 9. O něm (prep.) nic nevím. 10. Večeřeli jsem u nich (gen.) doma. 11. Chcete jít s námi (inst.) do restaurace?


**2. Translate.**
1. Peter was with us yesterday. 2. My sister didn't want to go to Prague with me. 3. Have you seen him? 4. Do you have the book with you? 5. How do you like Prague? 6. Do you understand him? 7. I didn't see you there. 8. Give it to them. 9. Does he need anything from us?

**3. Replace singular possessive pronouns with plural possessive pronouns and vice versa.**
1. Je tvoje sestra doma? 2. Vedle naší školy je knihovna. 3. Můj otec a moje matka šli na večeři. 4. To je její kniha. 5. Jejich adresu neznám. 6. Byl jsem v kině s jeho bratrem. 7. Je to jablko tvoje nebo moje? 8. Pojedete jejich autem? 9. Je tam s naší babičkou. 10. Váš dům má hnědou barvu.

**4. Translate.**
1. Do you know their address? 2. This is our first visit. 3. My wife is a teacher. 4. Your passports, please. 5. Is this his suitcase? 6. This is her house. 7. Your room is on the third floor. 8. My brother and his sister attend Charles University. 9. Our car is blue. 10. I want to hear about their vacation.

**5. *Translate into English.***
1. Nikdo nic neví. 2. Je někdo doma? 3. Nikdy ho nemohu najít. 4. Je tady nějaká restaurace? 5. S nikým nemusím mluvit. 6. Nemán žádnou knihu. 7. Ona bydlí někde v Praze.

**6. *Conversation.***
1. Kam jdou Horákovi a Novákovi na večeři?
2. Mají zamluvený stůl?
3. Co si objedná Eva?
4. Co se jich ptá číšník po jídle?
5. Kdo platí účet?

# Lesson 7

NA NÁKUPU

V obchodním domě.

Eva a Josef chtějí jít na nákup do obchodního domu Kotva.

Eva:            Pospěš si, Josefe! Obchodní dům zavírá v 6 hodin a
                jestli to nestihneme, budeme se muset vrátit zítra po
                desáté ráno.

Eva:            Dobrý večer. Chtěli bychom koupit letní oblek pro
                manžela.
Prodavačka:     Jakou máte velikost, pane?
Josef:          40 nebo 42, nejsem si jistý.
Prodavačka:     V těch velikostech máme bílý, béžový nebo světle
                modrý.
Josef:          Máte ho také v šedé?
Prodavačka:     Ano, ale ten vám bude asi malý. Chcete si ho
                vyzkoušet? Tamhle je kabinka.
Josef:          Děkuji. Ten oblek mi padne. Kolik stojí?
Prodavačka:     6400 korun. Platit budete u pokladny.
Josef:          Děkuji.
Eva:            Můžete nám říci, kde je oddělení obuvi?
Prodavačka:     Tamhle, hned za vámi.

V oddělení obuvi.

Prodavačka:     Co si přejete?
Eva:            Chtěla bych černé lodičky číslo 38.
Prodavačka:     Ty jsou vystaveny zde.
Eva:            Děkuji. Chtěla bych si tyto vyzkoušet.
Prodavačka:     Je mi líto, ale tyhle nemáme ve vaší velikosti. Chtěla
                byste si je vyzkoušet v jiné barvě?

Eva:               Ne, děkuji. Potřebuji černé lodičky. Zkusím se
                   podívat v jiném obchodě.


## SHOPPING

In a Department Store.

Eva and Josef want to go shopping at the department store Kotva.

Eva:               Hurry up, Josef! The department store closes at 6
                   p.m. and if we are late, we will have to go back
                   tomorrow after 10 a.m.

Eva:               Good evening. We would like to buy a summer suit
                   for my husband.
Clerk:             What is your size, sir?
Josef:             40 or 42, I am not sure.
Clerk:             In those sizes we have white, beige, or light blue.
Josef:             Do you have it in gray, too?
Clerk:             Yes, but it might be too small for you. Would you
                   like to try it on? The fitting room is over there.
Josef:             Thank you. The suit fits fine. How much is it?
Clerk:             6400 crowns. You pay at the cash register.
Josef:             Thank you.
Eva:               Can you tell us where the shoe department is?
Clerk:             Over there, right behind you.

At the Shoe Department.

Clerk:             May I help you? (lit.: What do you wish?)
Eva:               I would like a  pair of black dress shoes in size 38.
Clerk:             They are displayed right here.
Eva:               Thank you. I would like to try these on.
Clerk:             I am sorry, but we do not have those in your size.
                   Would you like to try them on in another color?
Eva:               No, thank you. I need a pair of black dress shoes. I
                   will try some other store.

## VOCABULARY

| | |
|---|---|
| béžový | beige |
| bota | shoe |
| bunda | jacket |
| dál | further |
| dívat se/podívat se | to watch/to look |
| dlouhý | long |
| drahý | expensive |
| halenka | blouse |
| hezký | pretty |
| hluboký | deep |
| chytrý | smart |
| jestli | if |
| kabinka | fitting room |
| kalhoty (pl.) | pants |
| košile (f.) | shirt |
| krásný | beautiful |
| krátký | short |
| lehký | light |
| lidský | human (adj.) |
| lodičky (pl.) | dress shoes |
| měkký | soft |
| najít | to find |
| nákup | shopping |
| než | than |
| oblečení | clothes |
| oblek | suit |
| obuv | shoes/shoe department |
| oddělení | department (noun) |
| ošklivý | ugly |
| padnout | to fit, to suit |
| pilný | diligent/hard-working |
| pokladna | cash register |
| pomáhat/pomoci | to help |
| pomalu | slowly |
| pomalý | slow |
| pomoc (f., kost) | help |
| poslouchat (imp.) | to listen |
| pospíchat (imp.) | to hurry |
| praktický | practical |

| | |
|---|---|
| rozejít se | to split up/to go separate ways |
| rozhodující | determining |
| rusky | Russian (adv.) |
| ruský | Russian (adj.) |
| sako | sports jacket |
| sedmý | seventh |
| silný | strong |
| snadný | easy |
| spěchat (imp.) | to hurry |
| stihnout | to make it on time |
| studený | cold |
| světle | light (adv.) |
| světlý | light (adj.) |
| šaty (pl.) | dress |
| široký | wide |
| tamhle | over there |
| těžký | heavy/difficult |
| tichý | quiet |
| tričko | T-shirt |
| tvrdý | hard |
| úzký | narrow |
| velikost (f., kost) | size |
| vracet/vrátit | to return |
| všechen (pron.) | all |
| vysoký | tall |
| vystavovat/vystavit | to display |
| vyzkoušet | to try on |
| zavírat/zavřít | to close |
| zkoušet/zkusit | to try |

## EXPRESSIONS

| | |
|---|---|
| Pospěš si! | Hurry up! |
| Co si přejete? | May I help you? (in a store) |

**GRAMMAR**

## 1. Adverbs

Most of the adverbs are formed from adjectives. They are created as follows:

a) The -ý or -í ending of the adjective is dropped and **-e** or **-ě** is added.
   *Example*:
   mladý - mladě, jarní - jarně, dobrý - dobře

b) The -cký, -ský, or -zký endings are shortened.
   *Example*:
   anglický - anglicky, ruský - rusky, hezký - hezky

c) The -ý ending from adjectives that end with -ký, -hý, or -chý is dropped and **-o, -e,** or **-ě** is added.
   *Example*:
   daleký - daleko, dalece; dlouhý - dlouho, dlouze

   Dlouho jsme na něj čekali.      We waited for him a long time.
   Dlouze se zamyslel.             He thought for a long time.

Note:
Be aware of stem changes.

## 2. Imperative

The imperative is used when we urge the person addressed to perform an action. It may be expressed in the form of a command, warning, request, etc.
*Example*:
Mluv česky!          Speak Czech!
Poslouchej!          Listen!

The imperative is created from the 3rd person plural by dropping its ending and adding proper imperative ending.

*Example:*

| infinitive | 3rd person pl. | imperative |
|---|---|---|
| mluvit | mluví | mluv/mluvme/mluvte! |
| číst | čtou | čti/čtěme/čtěte! |

Note:
The personal pronoun is not used.

There are two types of imperatives:
1. short imperative
2. long imperative

### 2.1 Short Imperative

The short imperative is used with verbs which after removing the final -í/-ou in the 3rd person plural end with a single consonant (mluví - mluv!). The forms are created as follows: root of the 3rd person pl. plus imperative endings.

| SHORT IMPERATIVE ENDINGS | | |
|---|---|---|
| **2nd person singular** | **1st person plural** | **2nd person plural** |
| *root + zero ending* | *root + -me* | *root + -te* |
| mluv | mluvme | mluvte |
| kup | kupme | kupte |
| studuj | studujme | studujte |
| pij | pijme | pijte |

Note:
1. If the present tense of the 3rd person plural ends with -ají, -a- is changed to -e- (dělají → dělej!).
2. If the present tense of the 3rd person plural ends with -í/-ou, the vowel in the syllable preceding the ending is shortened (píší → piš!, koupí → kup!).
3. If the exposed consonant is -d, -t, -n, it changes to -ď, -ť, -ň (sedí → seď!).

---

## 2.2  Long Imperative

The long imperative is used with verbs which after removing the ending of the 3rd person plural (-í or -ou) usually end with two or more consonants (čtou - čti!). The forms are created as follows: root of the 3rd person pl. plus imperative endings.

| LONG IMPERATIVE ENDINGS | | |
|---|---|---|
| **2nd person singular** | **1st person plural** | **2nd person plural** |
| *root* + *-i* | *root* + *-eme/-ěme* | *root* + *-ete/-ěte* |
| čti | čtěme | čtěte |
| jdi | jděme | jděte |
| řekni | řekněme | řekněte |
| mysli | mysleme | myslete |

Note:
If the stem ends with -d, -t, -n, then the -ěme/-ěte form is used.

## 2.3  Irregular Imperatives

| | | |
|---|---|---|
| jíst | - | jez! |
| mít | - | měj! |
| pomoci | - | pomoz! |
| odpovědět | - | odpověz! |

The verb *být* also has an irregular form. It uses the future tense:
buď - buďme - buďte

## 3.  Comparison of Adjectives

Most Czech adjectives can be expressed in three degrees:
a)  positive: mladý (young)
b)  comparative: mladší (younger)
c)  superlative: nejmladší (youngest)

The comparative and superlative adjectives end with the ending **-í**. They are declined as the soft adjectives *(pattern jarní)*.

<u>Comparative (second degree) adjectives</u> are formed by adding one of three suffixes **-ejší/-ější** *(nový - novější)*, **-ší** *(tvrdý - tvrdší)*, or **-í** *(hezký - hezčí)* to the stem.

The endings are added based upon the following rules:

-ejší/ější: - majority of adjectives with hard stem
- adjectives with soft stem

-ší: - limited number of adjectives, especially adjectives that end with -oký/-eký (they lose -ok-/-ek- in comparison: hluboký - hlubší)

-í: - adjectives ending with -ký

<u>Note</u>:
Please be aware of stem changes. Also, for accuracy check the Czech language dictionary since the rules have <u>many</u> exceptions.

<u>Superlative (third degree) adjectives</u> are formed from second degree adjectives by adding the prefix **nej-** *(nejnovější)*.

### 3.1 Consonant Change

Some adjectives undergo consonant changes when used in comparative and/or superlative form.

| CONSONANT CHANGE | | |
|---|---|---|
| Before the suffix -ší | | |
| ch | š | tichý - tišší |
| h | ž | drahý - dražší |
| z | ž | úzký - užší |
| s | š | vysoký - vyšší |
| d | z | snadný - snazší |

| CONSONANT CHANGE | | |
|---|---|---|
| Before the suffix **-ejší** | | |
| sk | šť | lidský - lidštější |
| ck | čť | praktický - praktičtější |
| r | ř | chytrý - chytřejší |
| k | č | křepký - křepčí/křepčejší |
| h | ž | strohý - strožejší |
| Before the suffix **-í** | | |
| k | č | hezký - hezčí |

Note:
The long syllable is shortened before adding the suffix **-ší**.

## 3.2 Irregularities

Adjectives which express a feature use other words to increase their degree. They use words such as: více (more), nejvíce (most), mnohem (a lot), velmi (very), zcela (totally).

*Example*:
rozhodující, více rozhodující, nejvíce rozhodující

| IRREGULAR COMPARISONS | | |
|---|---|---|
| **1st degree** | **2nd degree** | **3rd degree** |
| dlouhý | delší | nejdelší |
| dobrý | lepší | nejlepší |
| malý | menší | nejmenší |
| špatný | horší | nejhorší |
| velký | větší | největší |

Note:
*Více* (more) and *nejvíce* (the most) are second and third degree

forms of the adverb *hodně* (a lot) or *mnoho* (many).

## 3.3 Comparison of Two Subjects

When comparing two subjects the conjunction **než** is used.
*Example:*
Jana je starší než Petr.    Jana is older than Peter.

## 3.4 Comparison of Subject and Object

The preposition **z** and **genitive** case is used.
*Example:*
Jana je z nás nejstarší.    Jana is the oldest among us.

## 4. Pronoun All (Všechen)

| DECLENSION OF THE PRONOUN "VŠECHEN" | | | | |
|---|---|---|---|---|
| case | m. anim. | m. inanim. | f. | n. |
| **singular** | | | | |
| 1. | všechen | všechen | všechna | všechno |
| 2. | všeho | všeho | vší | všeho |
| 3. | všemu | všemu | vší | všemu |
| 4. | všeho | všechen | všechnu | všechno |
| 6. | všem | všem | vší | všem |
| 7. | vším | vším | vší | vším |
| **plural** | | | | |
| 1. | všichni | všechny | všechny | všechna |
| 2. | všech | všech | všech | všech |
| 3. | všem | všem | všem | všem |
| 4. | všechny | všechny | všechny | všechna |

| 6. | všech | všech | všech | všech |
| 7. | všemi | všemi | všemi | všemi |

## EXERCISES

1. *Change the following adjectives to adverbs.*
   Mladý, pilný, zimní, hlavní, anglický, pražský, sladký, nový, dlouhý, úzký, široký, starý, rychlý, silný, dobrý, červený.

2. *Put verbs in parentheses into the imperative form (where possible use also 1st and 2nd person plural).*
   1. (Čekat) před školou. 2. (Číst) pomalu. 3. (Nespěchat), máme čas. 4. (Pracovat) pilně. 5. (Mluvit) jenom česky. 6. Jano, (nepít) studenou vodu. 7. Petře, (napsat) ten dopis. 8. (Koupit) v obchodě mléko a chleba. 9. (Zaplatit) ten účet.

3. *Put the following adjectives into second or third degree comparisons.*
   1. Petr je (vysoký) než Pavel. 2. Moje sestra je (hezký) než já. 3. Jan je (chytrý) ze všech studentů. 4. Petr je (rychlý) než Pavel, ale Václav je (rychlý). 5. Petrova bunda je (teplý) než moje, ale Janina je (teplý). 6. Tato halenka je (drahý) než tahle. 7. Tato kniha je má (milý). 8. Tvoje auto je (dobrý) než moje. 9. Petr je ze všech (malý). 10. Kdo je (praktický), Jana nebo Eva? 11. Praha je (velký) z našich měst.

4. *Conversation.*
   1. Kam Eva a Josef spěchají?
   2. V kolik hodin zavírá obchodní dům Kotva?
   3. Jakou má Josef velikost?
   4. V jakých barvách mají oblek pro Josefa?
   5. Co si chce koupit Eva?

# Lesson 8

NA NÁVŠTĚVĚ

Pozvání na večeři.

Jana:     Horákovi nás dnes pozvali na večeři.
Václav:   To je od nich hezké. V kolik hodin?
Jana:     V 7 hodin. Musíme vyjet dříve, protože jim
          potřebujeme koupit dárek. Také bychom měli být na čas.
Václav:   Co jim chceš koupit?
Jana:     Květiny, láhev vína a čokoládu pro jejich děti. Pospěš si,
          za 10 minut musíme odejít.

U Horáků doma. Zvonek zvoní.

Eva:      Jana s Václavem jsou tady. Josefe, otevři dveře, prosím.
Josef:    Ahoj. Pojďte dál. Měli jste problém najít náš dům?
Václav:   Ne, bylo to snadné, protože jsme jeli taxíkem. Tady jsou
          květiny pro Evu a láhev vína pro tebe. Kde jsou děti?
Eva:      Děti jsou u babičky. Ty květiny jsou nádherné, děkuji.
Josef:    Co byste chtěli pít?
Jana:     Já si dám gin s tonikem.
Václav:   Pro mě taky.
Josef:    Pojďte, ukáži vám náš byt. Není velký, ale je pohodlný.
          Tady je ložnice a dětský pokoj a tady je koupelna.
          Kuchyň je tam a obývací pokoj je zde vpravo.
Václav:   Něco tu krásně voní. Co je to?
Eva:      Připravila jsem tradiční české jídlo: slepičí vývar s
          nudlemi, vepřovou pečeni se zelím a knedlíky a ovocný
          koláč jako zákusek.
Jana:     To zní dobře!

Po večeři.

Václav:   Trochu jsem se přejedl, ale všechno bylo výborné.

| Eva: | Děkuji. |
| Eva: | Není zač. Přejděme do obývacího pokoje. |
| Jana: | Evo, já ti pomohu sklidit se stolu. |
| Eva: | To počká, ale šampaňské nepočká. |

O dvě hodiny později.

| Václav: | Už je pozdě. Musíme jít. Josefe, mohl bys nám, prosím, zavolat taxíka? |
| Josef: | Samozřejmě. (Vytáčí číslo.) Dobrý večer. Mohli byste poslat taxíka do Plzeňské ulice číslo 25, byt na jméno Horák? Telefonní číslo 565632. Děkuji. Taxík tu bude za 15 minut. |
| Jana: | Děkujeme za krásný večer a vaši pohostinnost. Na shledanou. |
| Václav: | Dobrou noc. |
| Eva,Josef: | Na shledanou. Dobrou noc. |

## BEING A GUEST

Dinner Invitation.

| Jana: | The Horáks invited us for dinner today. |
| Václav: | That's nice of them. What time? |
| Jana: | At 7 o'clock. We have to leave earlier because we need to buy them a gift. Also, we should be there on time. |
| Václav: | What do you want to buy for them? |
| Jana: | Flowers, bottle of wine, and some chocolate for their children. Hurry up, we have to leave in 10 minutes. |

At the Horáks'. The bell rings.

| Eva: | Jana and Václav are here. Josef, open the door, please. |
| Josef: | Hello! Come in, please. Did you have trouble finding our house? |
| Václav: | No, it was easy because we took a taxi. Here are some flowers for Eva and a bottle of wine for you. Where are the children? |
| Eva: | They are at grandmother's. The flowers are beautiful, thank you. |

| | |
|---|---|
| Josef: | What would you like to drink? |
| Jana: | I will have a gin and tonic. |
| Václav: | Me too. |
| Josef: | Let me show you our apartment. It is not big, but it is comfortable. Here is the master bedroom and the kids' bedroom and here is the bathroom. The kitchen is there and the living room is here on the right. |
| Václav: | Something smells very good here. What is it? |
| Eva: | I have prepared a traditional Czech dinner: chicken soup with noodles, roast pork with sauerkraut and dumplings, and fruit cake for dessert. |
| Jana: | That sounds great! |

After Dinner.

| | |
|---|---|
| Václav: | I ate too much, but everything was delicious. Thank you. |
| Eva: | You are welcome. Let's go to the living room. |
| Jana: | Eva, I will help you clean the table. |
| Eva: | It will wait, but the champagne will not. |

Two Hours Later.

| | |
|---|---|
| Václav: | It is late. We must go. Josef, could you call a taxi for us, please? |
| Josef: | Of course. (He dials the number.) Good evening. Could you send a taxi to Pilsen Street 25, Horák apartment? The phone number is 565632. Thank you. The taxi will be here in 15 minutes. |
| Jana: | Thank you for a wonderful evening and your hospitality. Good-bye. |
| Václav: | Good night. |
| Eva,Josef: | Good-bye. Good night. |

## VOCABULARY

| | |
|---|---|
| aby | in order to |
| byt | apartment |
| čistý | clean |
| čokoláda | chocolate |
| dětský pokoj | children's room/bedroom |

| | |
|---|---|
| dovést | to be able to/ to know how |
| dříve | earlier |
| dveře (pl.) | door |
| hloupý | dumb, stupid |
| hrát (imp.) | to play |
| chodba | hallway |
| kdyby | if |
| kočka | cat |
| koláč | fruit cake |
| koupelna | bathroom |
| krásně | beautifully |
| kuchyň | kitchen |
| kuchyně | (ethnic) food |
| květina | flower |
| láhev (f., kolej) | bottle |
| líný | lazy |
| ložnice | bedroom/master bedroom |
| lyžovat (imp.) | to ski |
| mapa | map |
| nádherný | beautiful |
| nízký | short |
| nudle (f., růže) | noodle |
| obývací pokoj | living room |
| odcházet/odejít | to leave (on foot) |
| odlet | departure (by plane) |
| okno | window |
| osmý | eighth |
| ovocný | fruit (adj.) |
| pes | dog |
| počítat (imp.) | to count, to compute |
| pohostinnost | hospitality |
| potom | after/then |
| pozdě | late (adv.) |
| pozdní | late (adj.) |
| pozvání | invitation |
| pracovitý | hard-working |
| problém | problem |
| protože | because |
| přejíst se | to eat too much |
| přesunovat/přesunout | to move |
| připravovat/připravit | to prepare |

| | |
|---|---|
| řada | row |
| slepičí vývar/polévka | chicken soup |
| smět | to be allowed to |
| sklízet/sklidit | to clean |
| spojený | connected |
| stávat se/stát se | to happen |
| šampaňské (víno) | champagne |
| špinavý | dirty |
| taky | also |
| tonik | tonic (water) |
| tradice | tradition |
| tradiční | traditional |
| trochu | little bit |
| umět | to know how |
| už/již | already |
| věta | sentence, clause |
| vonět (imp.) | to smell (good) |
| vyjíždět/vyjet | to drive out, to leave (by transportation) |
| záchod | toilet, rest room |
| země (f.) | country/earth/the Earth |
| znít (imp.) | to sound |
| zvát/pozvat | to invite |
| zvonek | bell |
| zvonit/zazvonit | to ring |

## EXPRESSIONS

| | |
|---|---|
| Pojďte dál. | Come in. |
| Už je pozdě. | It is late. |

**GRAMMAR**

## 1. Modal Verbs

| CONJUGATION OF MODAL VERBS | | | | |
|---|---|---|---|---|
| **chtít** | **moci** | **muset** | **smět** | **umět** |
| present tense | | | | |
| já | chci | mohu | musím | smím | umím |
| ty | chceš | můžeš | musíš | smíš | umíš |
| on | chce | může | musí | smí | umí |
| my | chceme | můžeme | musíme | smíme | umíme |
| vy | chcete | můžete | musíte | smíte | umíte |
| oni | chtějí | mohou | musejí | smějí | umějí |
| past tense | | | | |
| on | chtěl | mohl | musel | směl | uměl |

Note:
The verb "mít" besides its basic meaning "to have" also has a modal
meaning.

## 2. Conditional Mood

### 2.1 Conditional Form of To Be (Být)

| CONDITIONAL FORM OF THE VERB "BÝT" | | |
|---|---|---|
| **person** | **singular** | **plural** |
| 1st | bych | bychom |
| 2nd | bys | byste |
| 3rd | by | by |

Note:

With reflexive pronouns *se* and *si* the form is *by ses* and *by sis* (2nd person sing.).
*Example:*
Chtěl by sis hrát?            Would you like to play?
Chtěla by ses dívat?          Would you like to watch?

**2.2  Conditional Form of "Kdyby"**
Kdyby means "if" and is used in conditional clauses like in English. Its form depends upon the subject of the sentence. For further information see paragraph 2.6 in this lesson.

| CONDITIONAL FORM OF "KDYBY" | | |
|---|---|---|
| **person** | **singular** | **plural** |
| 1st | kdybych | kdybychom |
| 2nd | kdybys | kdybyste |
| 3rd | kdyby | kdyby |

**2.3  Present Conditional**

The present conditional mood is formed as follows:

| Past Tense of the Meaning Verb | + | Conditional Form of "Být" |
|---|---|---|

*Example:*
Chtěl bych jít do kina.        I would like to go to the cinema.
Mohl bych vám pomoci?          Could I help you?
Pomohl by nám, ale...          He would help us, but...

The conditional mood is also used for a polite request. Note the hierarchy of politeness in the following sentences.
*Example:*
Zavolej mu.                    Call him.
Zavoláš mu?                    Will you call him?
Zavolal bys mu?                Would you call him?

Nezavolal bys mu?    Wouldn't you call him?

## 2.4  Past Conditional

The past conditional mood is formed as follows:

| Past Tense of "Být" | + | Conditional Form of "Být" | + | Past Tense of the Meaning Verb |
|---|---|---|---|---|

*Example:*
Byl bych vám pomohl.    I would have helped you.

## 2.5  Conditional Clauses

a) Real
Když je teplo, Petr jezdí    If it is warm, Peter rides his
na kole.    bike.

Note:
The tenses in the Czech sentences are the same as in English.

b) Unreal
Kdyby jel Petr na kole,    If Peter rode his bike,
byl by doma včas.    he would be at home on time.

Note:
Both Czech sentences use the conditional form, while in English
past tense is used in the dependent clause and conditional form
is used in the independent clause.

c) Past
Kdybychom tam byli šli,    If we had gone there,
nestalo by se to.    it would not have happened.

Note:
Czech:    Dependent clause: past conditional.
Independent clause: conditional.
English:  Dependent clause: past perfect tense.
Independent clause: past conditional.

## 2.6   Contrary to Fact Statements

These statements start with **kdyby** which means "if."
*Example*:

| | |
|---|---|
| Kdybychom tam šli, nestalo by se to. | If we went there, it would not happen. |
| Kdybychom tam byli šli, bylo by se to nestalo. | If we had gone there, it would not have happened. |

## 2.7   Use of "Aby"

"Aby" is used in indirect commands, requests, etc.
Based upon the subject of the sentence its form is as follows:

| CONDITIONAL FORM OF "ABY" | | |
|---|---|---|
| **person** | **singular** | **plural** |
| 1st | abych | abychom |
| 2nd | abys | abyste |
| 3rd | aby | aby |

*Example:*

| | |
|---|---|
| Pospěš si, abychom nebyli pozdě. | Hurry, so that we are not late. |
| Chci, abys tam šel. | I want you to go there. |

"Aby" is also used in the place of "in order to".
*Example*:

| | |
|---|---|
| Abyste to našli, musíte mít mapu. | In order for you to find it you must have a map. |

## 3.   Ordinal Numerals

Ordinal numerals are in most cases formed by adding **-ý** to cardinal numerals (*šest - šestý*). In addition to adding the ending, some numerals undergo stem changes (*deset - desátý*) and some have irregular forms (*jeden - první*). The cardinal numerals are declined as hard or soft adjectives (pattern *mladý*, pattern *jarní*) and must

agree with the noun they modify.
*Example*:
První žena, druhé dítě, devátý syn, etc.

| | | | |
|---|---|---|---|
| 1. | první | 11. | jedenáctý |
| 2. | druhý | 20. | dvacátý |
| 3. | třetí | 21. | dvacátý první |
| 4. | čtvrtý | 30. | třicátý |
| 5. | pátý | 40. | čtyřicátý |
| 6. | šestý | 50. | padesátý |
| 7. | sedmý | 100. | stý |
| 8. | osmý | 1000. | tisící |
| 9. | devátý | | |
| 10. | desátý | | |

Note:
1. When using a combined number, both numbers are in the ordinal form.
*Example*:
Dvacátá třetí kniha. Twenty-third book.
2. A cardinal numeral followed by a period is read as an ordinal numeral.
*Example*:
1. - první, 15. - patnáctý, etc.

**EXERCISES**
1. *Put the following modal verbs in the right form of present tense.*
1. (Muset-1st p. sing.) jít na poštu. 2. (Muset-2nd p. sing.) jít do školy. 3. (Chtít-2nd p. pl.) jít do kina? 4. (Smět-1st p. sing.) se vás na něco zeptat? 5. (Umět-2nd p. pl.) lyžovat? 6. (Chtít se-3rd p. pl.) učit česky.

2. *Put the following sentences into the conditional form.*
*Example*:
Jana nešla do obchodu. Jana nekoupila mléko.
Kdyby šla Jana do obchodu, koupila by mléko.

1. Petr nejel do Prahy. Petr nešel do kina. 2. Nebyli jsme doma. Neposlouchali jsme hudbu. 3. Nepomohli mi. Nedal jsem jim

peníze. 4. Nepřišel jsi. Nedostal jsi večeři. 5. Nezavolali jste mi. Nesešli jsme se.

3. *Use "aby" in the following sentences.*
*Example*: Poslouchej mě. Chci, abys mě poslouchal.

1. Kup to. 2. Zavolejte mi. 3. Dej mi tu knihu. 4. Představme se. 5. Jdi do kina. 6. Čekej na mě před školou.

4. *Use ordinal numerals.*
a) Dnes máme 4. lekci. b) Čtěte 9. větu. c) Dnes je 13. dubna. d) Narodila jsem se ve 20. století. e) Narodilo se jim 3. dítě. f) Sedíme v 5. řadě. g) Zítra bude 27. května. h) Včera bylo 31. srpna. ch) Petr chodí do 7. třídy. i) Tohle je můj 2. manžel.

5. *Find antonyms for the following adjectives.*

| | |
|---|---|
| vysoký | chytrý |
| pracovitý | starý |
| malý | tvrdý |
| sladký | těžký |
| otevřený | krátký |
| čistý | hezký |

6. *Conversation.*
1. Jaké dárky koupili Novákovi Horákům?
2. Kde jsou Horákovy děti?
3. Co si Václav s Evou dají k pití?
4. Co připravila Eva k večeři?
5. Kde pijí všichni šampaňské?

# Lesson 9

## ZDRAVOTNÍ OŠETŘENÍ

Brzy ráno v pokoji v hotelu.

| | |
|---|---|
| Václav: | Jano, není mi dnes dobře. Nevím, co mi je. |
| Jana: | Jsi bledý. Máš nějaké bolesti? |
| Václav: | Bolí mě břicho a hlava a začínám mít závratě. |
| Jana: | Zavolám na recepci, aby sem poslali lékaře. |
| Lékař: | Dobré ráno. Jsem doktor Pavel Hájek. Co vás bolí? |
| Jana: | Můj manžel se necítí dobře. Bolí ho břicho a hlava. |
| Lékař: | Prosím, posaďte se. Změřím vám teplotu a krevní tlak. Máte zvýšenou teplotu - 37.4°C. Váš krevní tlak je normální. Kde vás bolí břicho? Tady? Otevřete ústa. Děkuji. Máte žaludeční nevolnost. Co jste včera jedl? |
| Václav: | Přejedl jsem se. Měli jsme večeři u známých doma. |
| Lékař: | Vypadá to, že už nejste zvyklý na českou kuchyni. Jsou to výborná jídla, ale těžká do žaludku. Alespoň dva dny musíte držet dietu. Pijte hořký čaj a jezte suchý chleba a rýži. Pozítří budete v pořádku. Zavolejte mi, jestliže se váš stav zhorší. Na shledanou. |
| Václav: | Děkuji. Na shledanou. |

### MEDICAL CARE

Early morning at the hotel room.

| | |
|---|---|
| Václav: | Jana, I am not feeling well today. I do not know what is wrong with me. |
| Jana: | You look pale. Do you have any pain? |
| Václav: | I have a stomach ache and a headache and I am starting to feel dizzy. |
| Jana: | I will call the front desk to ask for a doctor. |

| | |
|---|---|
| Doctor: | Good morning. I am Doctor Pavel Hájek. What is the problem? (lit.: What is hurting?) |
| Jana: | My husband is not feeling well. He has a stomach ache and a headache. |
| Doctor: | Please, sit up. I will take your temperature and blood pressure. You have a slight fever of 37.4°C. Your blood pressure is normal. Where does your stomach hurt? Here? Open your mouth. Thank you. You have an upset stomach. What did you eat yesterday? |
| Václav: | I ate too much. We had dinner at our friends' house. |
| Doctor: | It seems that you are not used to Czech food anymore. It is delicious, but very heavy for the stomach. You need to be on a diet for the next two days. Drink plain tea and eat toast and rice. You will be fine the day after tomorrow. Call me if your condition gets worse. Good-bye. |
| Václav: | Thank you. Good-bye. |

## VOCABULARY

| | |
|---|---|
| alespoň | at least |
| během (prepos., gen.) | during |
| bledý | pale |
| bolest (f., kost) | pain |
| bolest hlavy | headache |
| bolestivý | painful |
| bolet (imp.) | to hurt/to have pain |
| brzo | early |
| brzy | early |
| břicho | abdomen |
| celý | whole |
| cítit (imp.) | to feel |
| dieta | diet |
| doktor/doktorka | doctor male/female |
| dovolení | permission |
| držet (imp.) | to hold |
| dýchat (imp.) | to breathe |
| hlava | head |
| hořký | bitter |
| kabátek | jacket |

| | |
|---|---|
| koleno | knee |
| kolo | bicycle |
| krev (f., kolej) | blood |
| krevní tlak | blood pressure |
| krk | neck |
| kuchyně | (ethnic) food |
| měřit/změřit | to measure |
| místo (prepos., gen.) | instead |
| nad (prepos., acc./prep.) | above |
| nemocnice (f.) | hospital |
| nemocný | sick/ill |
| nevolnost (f., kost) | discomfort |
| noha | foot/leg |
| normální | normal |
| nos | nose |
| noviny (pl.) | newspaper |
| obejít | to go around |
| obyvatel | inhabitant |
| odborník | expert |
| oddělit | to separate |
| oko/oči | eye/eyes |
| okolo (prepos., gen.) | around |
| ošetření | care (medical) |
| ošetřit | to give care |
| otáčet se (imp.) | to turn around |
| palec | thumb |
| po (prepos., prep.) | after |
| pokládat/položit | to put |
| posadit se | to sit down/up |
| pozítří | the day after tomorrow |
| pravidelně | regularly |
| pravidelný | regular |
| projít | to pass through |
| prst | finger |
| přečíst | to finish reading |
| přejít | to walk across |
| přijít | to come, to arrive on foot |
| pyžamo | pajama |
| rodina | family |
| ruka | hand |
| sejít se | to meet somewhere with sbd. |

| | |
|---|---|
| sestoupit | to go down |
| spolužák/spolužačka | classmate male/female |
| srdce (n.) | heart |
| stát/zastavit | to stop/to stand |
| stav | condition (medical) |
| strýc | uncle |
| suchý | dry |
| sval | muscle |
| svlékat se/svléknout se | to take off (clothes) |
| tělo | body |
| teplota | temperature |
| teta | aunt |
| ucho/uši | ear/ears |
| ústa (pl.) | mouth |
| viset (imp.) | to hang |
| vlasy (pl.) | hair |
| vstoupit | to enter |
| vyjít | to start walking |
| vypadat (imp.) | to look like |
| vzduch | air |
| záda | back |
| závrať (f., kost) | dizziness |
| zdraví | health |
| zdravotní | medical |
| zdravý | healthy |
| zhoršovat/zhoršit | to get worse |
| známí (noun - pl.) | friends |
| známý (adj./noun - sing.) | known/friend |
| zub | tooth |
| zvykat si/zvyknout si | to get used to |
| zvyklý | accustomed |
| zvýšená teplota | higher temperature |
| zvýšený | higher |
| žaludeční | stomach (adj.) |
| žaludek | stomach (noun) |

## EXPRESSIONS

| | |
|---|---|
| Není mi dobře. | I am not feeling well. |
| Bolí mě břicho (hlava). | I have a stomach ache (headache). |

Nemohu se dočkat.      I can hardly wait.

**GRAMMAR**

## 1. Prepositions

Below are listed the most commonly used prepositions and their basic meanings.

**PREPOSITIONS**

| Czech | English | Case | Example |
|-------|---------|------|---------|
| během | during | gen. | Zavolej mi během odpoledne. Call me during the afternoon. |
| bez, beze | without | gen. | Půjdu domů bez mého bratra. I will go home without my brother. |
| do | to | gen. | Jedu do Prahy. I am going to Prague. |
| | into | gen. | Dal jsem si peníze do kapsy. I put the money into my pocket. |
| | till | gen. | Čekali jsme až do večera. We waited till the evening. |
| k, ke, ku | to | dat. | Jdu k sestře. I am going to my sister's house. |
| | toward | dat. | Jedu ku Praze. I am going toward Prague. |
| mezi | between, among (dir.) | acc. | Sedni si tam - mezi matku a otce! Sit down over there - between your mother and father! |
| | between, among (loc.) | inst. | Jana sedí mezi matkou a otcem. Jana sits between her mother and father. |
| místo | instead of | gen. | Půjdu tam místo tebe. I will go there instead of you. |

| PREPOSITIONS | | | |
|---|---|---|---|
| **Czech** | **English** | **Case** | **Example** |
| na | on (dir.) | acc. | Dej knihu na stůl. Put the book on the table. |
| | on (loc.) | prep. | Kniha je na stole. The book is on the table. |
| nad | above (dir.) | acc. | Pověs obraz nad stůl. Hang the painting above the table. |
| | above (loc.) | inst. | Obraz visí nad stolem. The painting is hanging above the table. |
| naproti | opposite, across from | dat. | Sedím naproti Janě. I sit opposite Jana. |
| o | about | prep. | Čtu knihu o Praze. I am reading a book about Prague. |
| od, ode | from | gen. | Chci to od tebe. I want it from you. |
| | since | gen. | Jsem v Praze od ledna. I have been in Prague since January. |
| po | after | prep. | Po kině půjdu domů. I will go home after the movie. |
| pod | under (dir.) | acc. | Dej to pod stůl. Put it under the table. |
| pod | under (loc.) | inst. | Pes je pod stolem. The dog is under the table. |
| pro | for | acc. | Tato kniha je pro Janu. This book is for Jana. |
| před | in front of (dir.) | acc. | Postav se před sestru. Stand in front of my sister. |
| před | in front of (loc.) | inst. | Stojím před sestrou. I am standing in front of my sister. |
| přes | across | acc. | Jdu přes most. I am going across the bridge. |

| PREPOSITIONS | | | |
|---|---|---|---|
| **Czech** | **English** | **Case** | **Example** |
| s, se | with | inst. | Pracuji s Petrem. I work with Peter. |
| u | by | gen. | Jana stojí u okna. Jana is standing by the window. |
| | at | gen. | Sedíme u stolu. We are sitting at the table. |
| v, ve | in | prep. | Bydlím v Praze. I live in Prague. Jsem v museu. I am in a museum. |
| | at | prep. | Jsem ve škole. I am at school. |
| | on | acc. | V sobotu. On Saturday. |
| vedle | next to | gen. | Jana sedí vedle Petra. Jana is sitting next to Peter. |
| z, ze | from | gen. | Jsem z Ameriky. I am from America. |
| za | behind (dir.) | acc. | Postav se za sestru. Stand behind my sister. |
| | behind (loc.) | inst. | Stojím za sestrou. I am standing behind my sister. |

## 2. Prefixal Verbs

Prefixes very often modify the basic meaning of the verb. Listed below are such commonly used ones. They are simply added to the basic verbs.

*Example:*

číst (to read) -     **pře**číst (to finish reading)

jít (to go)     -     **při**jít (to come)

                      **ode**jít (to leave)

## PREFIXAL VERBS

| Prefix | Meaning | Example |
|---|---|---|
| při- | to, toward | Petr k nám **při**šel na návštěvu.<br>Peter came to visit us. |
| od-,<br>ode- | the opposite to<br>*při-*; away, off,<br>separation | Petr od nás **ode**šel.<br>Peter left us.<br>**Odd**ěl to. Separate it. |
| pro- | through | **Pro**šel jsem celým lesem.<br>I walked through the whole forest. |
| pře- | over, across<br><br>to finish an<br>activity | Petr **pře**šel řeku po mostě.<br>Peter walked across the river on a<br>bridge.<br>**Pře**četla jsem knížku.<br>I have read (finished reading) the<br>book. |
| s-, se- | down, off from the<br>surface | Petr **se**stoupil do prvního patra.<br>Peter went down to the first floor. |
| s-, se- | to bring together | **Se**jdeme se zítra. We will meet<br>tomorrow.<br>Petr **s**bírá známky. Peter collects<br>stamps. |
| v-,<br>ve- | in, to enter | Petr **v**stoupil do třídy.<br>Peter entered the classroom. |
| vy- | the opposite to *v-*;<br>the opposite of<br>entering, out | Petr **vy**stoupil z metra.<br>Peter got off the subway. |
| vy- | the opposite to *s-*;<br>up | Petr **vy**stoupil na vrchol.<br>Peter reached the top of the<br>mountain. |

### 2.1 Prefixal Verbs of the Root "Jít"

**obe**jít          to go around
**ode**jít          to leave

| projít | to pass through |
|---|---|
| přejít | to walk across |
| přijít | to come |
| rozejít se | to go separate ways |
| sejít se | to meet |
| vyjít | to start walking |
| zajít | to go to a place |

## 3. Possessive Adjectives

Possessive adjectives use in their basic form (masculine, nominative, singular) the following endings:
a) -ův: formed from masculine animate nouns
b) -in: formed from feminine nouns; representing the animate group

*Example:*

Petr - Petrův (Peter's)      Jana - Janin (Jana's)
bratr - bratrův (brother's)   sestra - sestřin (sister's)

Again, the adjective must agree with the modifying noun in terms of gender, number, and case.

### 3.1 Declension of Possessive Adjectives Ending with "-ův"

| POSSESSIVE ADJECTIVES ENDING WITH "-ův" | | | | |
|---|---|---|---|---|
| case | m. anim. | m. inanim. | f. | n. |
| singular | | | | |
| 1. | otcův | otcův | otcova | otcovo |
| 2. | otcova | otcova | otcovy | otcova |
| 3. | otcovu | otcovu | otcově | otcovu |
| 4. | otcova | otcův | otcovu | otcovo |
| 6. | otcově | otcově | otcově | otcově |
| 7. | otcovým | otcovým | otcovou | otcovým |

| POSSESSIVE ADJECTIVES ENDING WITH "-ův" | | | |
|---|---|---|---|
| case | m. anim. | m. inanim. | f. | n. |
| | | plural | | |
| 1. | otcovi | otcovy | otcovy | otcova |
| 2. | otcových | otcových | otcových | otcových |
| 3. | otcovým | otcovým | otcovým | otcovým |
| 4. | otcovy | otcovy | otcovy | otcova |
| 6. | otcových | otcových | otcových | otcových |
| 7. | otcovými | otcovými | otcovými | otcovými |

**3.2  Declension of Possessive Adjectives Ending with "-in"**

| POSSESSIVE ADJECTIVES ENDING WITH "-in" | | | |
|---|---|---|---|
| case | m. anim. | m. inanim. | f. | n. |
| | | singular | | |
| 1. | matčin | matčin | matčina | matčino |
| 2. | matčina | matčina | matčiny | matčina |
| 3. | matčinu | matčinu | matčině | matčinu |
| 4. | matčina | matčin | matčinu | matčino |
| 6. | matčině | matčině | matčině | matčině |
| 7. | matčiným | matčiným | matčinou | matčiným |

## POSSESSIVE ADJECTIVES ENDING WITH "-in"

| case | m. anim. | m. inanim. | f. | n. |
|---|---|---|---|---|
| | plural | | | |
| 1. | matčini | matčiny | matčiny | matčina |
| 2. | matčiných | matčiných | matčiných | matčiných |
| 3. | matčiným | matčiným | matčiným | matčiným |
| 4. | matčiny | matčiny | matčiny | matčina |
| 6. | matčiných | matčiných | matčiných | matčiných |
| 7. | matčinými | matčinými | matčinými | matčinými |

## EXERCISES

**1. Decline the following words using your knowledge about prepositions.**
1. Kniha je na (stůl). 2. Otec pracuje v (universitní knihovna). 3. Petr studuje češtinu s tou (nová studentka). 4. Sejdeme se u (Národní divadlo). 5. O (moderní cizí literatury) bylo málo přednášek. 6. Ráda čtu knihy o (daleká místa).

**2. Insert the right preposition.**
1. Byli jsme ... škole. 2. Auto zastavilo ... domem. 3. Jana stojí ... okna. 4. Chodím pravidelně ... lékaři. 5. Jana a Petr šli ... kina. 6. Přijď ... nám ... pátek ... třetí a čtvrtou hodinou. 7. Potřebuji ... tebou mluvit. 8. Přejdi ... ulici. 9. Knihovna je ... školy. 10. Škola je ... mostem. 11. Sedím ... Jany ... stolu. 12. Pes je ... stolem. 13. Obraz visí ... stolem.

**3. Change the nouns in parentheses into possessive adjectives and put them in the right form.**
1. Kde je (Petr - nom., sing.) kniha? 2. O (Josef - prep., sing.) bratrovi nikdo nic neví. 3. (Sestra - nom., sing.) přítel je můj spolužák. 4. Půjdu do kina s (Jana - inst., sing.) sestrou. 5. Před (Karel - inst., sing.) mostem je hodně lidí. 6. Nejezdi na (sestra - prep., sing.) kole. 7. Sedni si na (babička - acc., sing.) židli. 8.Jana sedí vedle (Josef - gen., sing.) přítele Karla. 9. Kolik stojí

tato (Havel - nom., sing.) kniha? 10. Bez (otec - gen., sing.) a (matka - gen., sing.) dovolení nikam nechod.

**4. Conversation.**
1. Co bolí Václava?
2. Kam volá Jana pro lékaře?
3. Co měří lékař Václavovi?
4. Jakou má Václav teplotu?
5. Co řekl lékař Václavovi?

# Lesson 10

## SPOLEČENSKÝ VEČÍREK

Na podnikové oslavě.

Novákovi jdou na podnikovou oslavu do domu pana Landy, ředitele
české pobočky firmy, pro kterou pan Novák pracuje. Pozvou také
Horákovi.

| | |
|---|---|
| Václav: | Pane Landa, rád bych vám představil naše české přátele - Josef Horák a jeho žena Eva. Jan Landa, ředitel naší české pobočky. |
| Pan Landa: | Těší mě. Co děláte, pane Horák? |
| Josef: | Jsem lékař. Pracujete s Václavem už dlouho? |
| Pan Landa: | Ne, před dvěma dny jsme teprve podepsali smlouvu. Začneme spolu pracovat až příští měsíc. Do té doby bychom měli mít vyřízené všechny písemné záležitosti. |
| Václav: | Naše firma ve Spojených státech vyrábí počítače, které budeme dovážet do České republiky. Naše pobočka tady bude psát software pro český trh. |
| Josef: | Jsem přesvědčen, že je to výborný nápad. Časově je to velmi příhodné, neboť takové vybavení tady teď nutně potřebujeme. Hodně štěstí! |
| Eva: | Už je pozdě. Měli bychom jít, Josef musí jít brzy ráno do práce. Děkujeme za pozvání. Byl to moc hezký večírek. |
| Jana: | Jsme rádi, že jste přišli. My musíme také brzy ráno vstávat. Naše letadlo odlétá v 10 hodin ráno a ještě nemáme zabaleno. |
| Václav: | Jsme rádi, že jsme vás poznali. Tady je má navštívenka. Příště, až budete mít v plánu cestu do Ameriky, zavolejte nám. Do té doby na shledanou. |
| Josef: | Vy máte naši adresu a telefonní číslo. Budeme čekat na váš dopis. Šťastnou cestu. |

# SOCIAL EVENT

<u>At a Business Party.</u>

The Nováks are going to a business party at the house of Mr.
Landa, the director of the Czech division of Mr. Novak's company.
They invite the Horáks to come along.

| | |
|---|---|
| Václav: | Mr. Landa, I would like to introduce our Czech friends - Josef Horák and his wife Eva. Jan Landa, the director of our Czech division. |
| Mr. Landa: | Nice to meet you. What do you do for a living Mr. Horák? |
| Josef: | I am a doctor. Have you been working with Václav for a long time? |
| Mr. Landa: | No, we only signed the agreement two days ago. We will start working together next month. By then we should have finished the paperwork. |
| Václav: | Our company in the United States makes computers which will be imported to the Czech Republic. Our division here will write the software for the Czech market. |
| Josef: | I am sure that this is an excellent idea. The timing is perfect because there is a great need for such equipment here. Good luck! |
| Eva: | It is late. We should be leaving, Josef has to go to work early. Thanks for inviting us. It was a nice party. |
| Jana: | Thank you for coming. We have to get up early, too. Our plane leaves at 10 a.m. and we have not packed yet. |
| Václav: | It is so nice to have met you. Here is my business card. Next time you plan to come to America, please give us a call. Until then. |
| Josef: | You have our address and telephone number. We will be waiting for your letter. Have a nice trip. |

## VOCABULARY

| | |
|---|---|
| balit/zabalit | to pack |
| běhat/běžet | to run |
| časově | timing/timely |
| dovážet (imp.) | to import |
| ekonomika | economics |
| firma | firm |
| Jaderské moře | Adriatic sea |
| navštívenka | business card |
| nutný | necessary |
| oslava | party/celebration |
| písemný | written |
| pobočka | division |
| podepisovat/podepsat | to sign |
| podnik | company |
| podnikový | company (adj.) |
| podpis | signature |
| přátelé (pl.) | friends |
| přesvědčen (short adj.) | convinced |
| přesvědčený (adj.) | convinced |
| příhodný | suitable |
| příroda | nature |
| přítel/přítelkyně | friend male/female |
| ředitel | director |
| slovanský | slavic |
| smlouva | agreement |
| software | software |
| spojení | connection |
| společenský | formal |
| společnost (f., kost) | society |
| spolu | together |
| telefonní | telephone (adj.) |
| trh | market |
| večírek | party/ (social) event |
| vodit/vést | to lead, to take |
| vozit/vézt | to carry (by transportation) |
| vstávat/vstát | to get up |
| vybavení | equipment |
| vyrábět (imp.) | to produce, to make |
| vyřídit | to take care of |

| vyřízený | taken care of |
|---|---|
| vyvážet/vyvézt | to export |
| záležitost (f. kost) | affair (business) |
| zůstávat/zůstat | to stay |

## EXPRESSIONS

| Šťastnou cestu. | Have a nice trip. |
|---|---|
| Do té doby ... | Until then ... |
| Jsem přesvědčen, že ... | I am sure that ... |
| Už je pozdě. | It is late. |

## GRAMMAR

### 1. Sentence Structure

Statement: A statement usually starts with a subject followed by a predicate. If a personal pronoun (that is not present but is understood) is the subject, the sentence starts with a verb.
*Example*:

| Petr je doma. | Peter is at home. |
|---|---|
| Je doma s babičkou. | He is home with his grandmother. |

Question: A question either starts with a verb followed by the subject, or with an interrogative word (e.g., co, kde, kdo, kolik) followed by a verb.
*Example*:

| Je Petr doma? | Is Peter at home? |
|---|---|
| Kdo je s Petrem doma? | Who is at home with Peter? |

### 1.1 Word Order

The Czech language puts any new information at the end of a sentence.
*Example*:
Kde bydlíš? Bydlím *v Americe.* (Where do you live? I live in America.)

V kolik hodin budete večeřet? Budeme večeřet *v šest hodin*. (At what time will you eat dinner? We will eat dinner at six o'clock.)
In continuous speech a sentence which follows, starts with what is known from the sentence before.
*Example*:
Jana píše dopis Evě. *V dopise píše* o dovolené u moře. *Letošní dovolenou* strávila u Jaderského moře. (Jana is writing a letter to Eva. In the letter she is writing about her vacation at a sea. Jana spent this year's vacation at the Adriatic sea.)

**2. Double Imperfective Verbs of Motion**

Some motion verbs may have two imperfective forms. One expresses habitual motion, repeated motion, or motion in various directions. The other one expresses motion in one specific direction.

| VERBS OF MOTION | | |
|---|---|---|
| **Imperfective - different directions** | **Imperfective - one direction** | **English Translation** |
| jezdit | jet | to go (by means of transportation), to drive |
| chodit | jít | to go (on foot), to walk |

*Example:*
Petr jezdí do školy autobusem každý den.
Petr právě jede do školy.
Eva chodí po lese.
Eva jde do obchodního domu.

Peter goes to school by bus every day.
Peter is now going to school.
Eva is walking in the woods.
Eva is going to the department store.

**3. Forming Adjectives from Nouns**

A large number of adjectives are formed by adding suffixes **-ský, -ní**

to the stem of the noun.
*Example*:

| noun | adjective |
|------|-----------|
| pán | pánský |
| muž | mužský |
| žena | ženský |
| město | městský |
| jaro | jarní |
| hrad | hradní |
| stroj | strojní |
| moře | mořský |

In most cases adjectives formed from masculine animate, feminine animate (pattern *žena*), and neuter (patterns *město* and *moře*) nouns end with **-ský**. Masculine inanimate, feminine expressing inanimate objects (pattern *žena*) and some neuter nouns (pattern *město*) end with **-ní**.

Note:
1. Some irregularities:
   Praha - pražský
   Amerika - americký
2. Notice the difference between the English and Czech capitalization rules.

4. **Short Adjectives**

Some adjectives can create short forms (in addition to the long ones - see Lesson 4). These forms are used to express predicate, while long forms usually express attribute.
*Example:*

| Chlapec je nemocen. | The boy is sick. |
|---|---|
| versus | |
| Nemocný chlapec. | The sick boy. |

The short forms usually express a temporary state or situation.
*Example:*

| Petr je nemocen. | Peter is sick. |
|---|---|
| versus | |
| Doktor říká, že Petr je | The Doctor says Peter is very ill. |

velmi nemocný.

As mentioned above, only a small number of adjectives have short forms. They are created from long adjectives and only nominative and sometimes accusative cases can be formed. The short adjectives are created by dropping the -ý ending from the nominative, singular, masculine noun and adding the following endings:

| singular | | | plural |
|---|---|---|---|
| **masculine** | **feminine** | **neuter** | -i/ -y/ -a |
| zero ending | -a | -o | |
| laskav | laskava | laskavo | laskavi/ -y/ -a |

Note:
1. Some short forms undergo certain changes.
   a) Short stem is changed into long stem.
   *Example:*
   zdravý → zdráv
   b) Fleeting -e- is added.
   *Example:*
   nemocný → nemocen
2. Some adjectives (e.g., rád/glad) have only short forms.
*Example:*
Jsem rád, že tě vidím.      I am glad to see you.
3. Also, some short adjectives are used in phrases and idiomatic expressions.
*Example:*
Petr je hotov udělat vše,      Peter is ready to do anything
aby tě přesvědčil.      in order to convince you.

**4.1 Frequently Used Short Adjectives**

| | | |
|---|---|---|
| hotový | - | hotov (ready) |
| jistý | - | jist (sure) |
| laskavý | - | laskav (kind) |
| mladý | - | mlád (young) |
| mrtvý | - | mrtev (dead) |

| | | |
|---|---|---|
| nemocný | - | nemocen (sick, ill) |
| povinný | - | povinen (obligated) |
| schopný | - | schopen (capable) |
| spokojený | - | spokojen (satisfied) |
| šťastný | - | šťasten (happy) |
| vinný | - | vinen (guilty) |
| zdravý | - | zdráv (healthy) |
| zvědavý | - | zvědav (curious) |

Note:
Notice different spelling of the forms:
- povinen (m.), povinna (f.), povinno (n.), povinni/-y/-a (pl.)
- vinen (m.), vinna (f.), vinno (n.), vinni/-y/-a (pl.)

## EXERCISES

**1. Match the right beginnings and endings of the sentences and put them into chronological order.**

| | |
|---|---|
| Petr píše | ve Spojených státech. |
| Mary bydlí | ve státě Texas. |
| Bydlí | dopis Mary. |
| Chodí tam | v Praze. |
| Mary tu učila | slovanské jazyky. |
| Petr se seznámil s Mary | na universitu. |
| Mary studuje | angličtinu. |

**2. Insert the right form of the verb jít or chodit.**
1. Robert ...... dnes do kina. ...... do kina velmi často. 2. Každý den (já)...... do práce včas, dnes ale ...... pozdě. 3. (Ty)...... dnes večer do divadla? 4. Jak často (ty)...... do divadla? 5. Jana ...... do páté třídy.

**3. Insert the right form of the verb jet or jezdit.**
1. Petr ...... každý rok na dovolenou k moři. 2. Já ...... tento týden do Prahy. 3. ...... do Prahy často, protože mám čas. 4. Já ...... často autem.

**4. Change the following nouns into adjectives and use them in short sentences.**

1. Město 2. Praha 3. student 4. třída 5. učitel 6. Amerika 7. lékař 8. slovo 9. stroj 10. dopis 11. zima 12. les 13. příroda 14. moře

**5. Translate the following sentences. Use short adjectives.**
1. The boy is sick. 2. Peter is ready. 3. Please, be so kind and close the door. 4. I am curious how it will end. 5. I am very satisfied.

**6. Conversation.**
1. Koho také pozvali Novákovi na podnikovou oslavu?
2. Kam jdou na společenský večírek?
3. Co vyrábí Václavova firma ve Spojených státech?
4. Co bude dělat jejich česká pobočka?
5. V kolik hodin odlétá Novákovo letadlo?

# Key to excercises

## Lesson 1.

1. 1. je 2. má 3. máme 4. jsou 5. je 6. jsou 7. máš 8. je

2. 1. Mám./Nemám. 2. Je./Není. 3. Je./Není. 4. Jsou./Nejsou. 5. Mám./Nemám. 6. Jsem./Nejsem. 7. Je./Není.

3. 1. Jak se jmenuješ/jmenujete? 2. Kde bydlíš/bydlíte? 3. Ahoj. 4. Na shledanou. 5. Dobré odpoledne. 6. Těší mě/nás. 7. Jmenuji se Václav Novák. 8. Promiň/Promiňte. 9. Co děláte?/Jaké je vaše zaměstnání?

4. 1. Nemluvím česky. 2. Eva není učitelka. 3. Neletím na služební cestu. 4. Nemám babičku. 5. Ten inženýr se nejmenuje Horák. 6. Dcera nehovoří s matkou. 7. Otec a syn nejsou lékaři.

## Lesson 2.

1. 
| | | |
|---|---|---|
| kontrola (f., žena) | slovo (n., město) | odpoledne(n.,moře) |
| republika (f.,žena) | student (m.,pán) | most (m.,hrad) |
| dárek (m.,hrad) | stůl (m.,hrad) | ráno (n.,město) |
| kniha (f.,žena) | zavazadlo (n.,město) | noc (f.,kost) |
| kufr (m.,hrad) | čas (m.,hrad) | židle (f.,růže) |
| pas (m.,hrad) | dítě (n.,kuře) | řidič(m.,muž) |
| pořádek (m.,hrad) | lekce (f.,růže) | místo(n.,město) |
| proclení (n.,stavení) | manžel (m.,pán) | letadlo(n.,město) |
| počítač (m.,stroj) | seznámení(n.,stavení) | škola (f.,žena) |
| pole (n., moře) | lékař (m., muž) | pec (f., růže) |

2. 1. škole 2. češtinu 3. mostu 4. růži 5. Prahy 6. knihu u stolu 7. mostem 8. slovo

3. 1. (Já) Jsem Američan/ka. 2. Bydlím v Texasu. 3. Jmenuji se .... 4. Mám knihu. 5. Škola je za mostem. 6. Vaše pasy, prosím. 7. Mluvíš/Mluvíte česky? 8. Narodil/-a jsem se tam.

## Lesson 3.

1. tiskne-tisknou (2)  dává-dávají (5)
   mluví-mluví (4)  slyší-slyší (4)
   pracuje-pracují (3)  mine-minou (2)
   bydlí-bydlí/bydlejí (4)  letí-letí (4)

   dá-dají (5)  kupuje-kupují(3)
   vidí-vidí (4)  nosí-nosí(4)
   rozumí-rozumějí (4)  studuje-studují(3)
   čte-čtou (1)  jmenuje se-jmenují se (3)

2. 1. mluví/mluvila/bude mluvit 2. píše/psala/bude psát 3. jedeme/jsme jeli/pojedeme 4. bydlíš/bydlel jsi/budeš bydlet 5. pracují/pracovali/budou pracovat 6. znáte/jste znali/budete znát 7. jdeme/jsme šli/půjdeme

3. 1. (Já) Bydlím ve Spojených státech. 2. Kde je zastávka taxi? 3. Petře, sejdeme se naproti kinu. 4. Zastavte, prosím! 5. Hodně štěstí. 6. To nevadí.

## Lesson 4.

1. 1. červenou 2. zelené 3. modrý 4. černém 5. žlutém 6. fialovou nebo bílou 7. zlatého 8. žluté 9. stříbrné 10. modrou, dobré 11. jarní 12. letní 13. podzimním 14. zimní 15. zlaté a červené, v podzimním

3. 1. tu 2. ten 3. tou 4. ta, tu, 5. tom 6. tom 7. toho 8. té 9. té 10. ta

4. Zelená, modrá, zlaté, žluté, zelený, červená, bílý.

## Lesson 5.

5. 1. druhou hodinou 2. páté třídě 3. Petrem 4. Američany 5. cizích jazycích

## Lesson 6.

1. 1. s námi 2. je 3. něm, ní 4. je 5. mě 6. vámi 7. vám 8. jim 9. nich 10. něj, ní 11. se mnou

2. 1. Petr byl s námi včera. 2. Moje sestra nechtěla jet do Prahy se mnou. 3. Viděl jsi ho? 4. Máš tu knihu s sebou? 5. Jak se ti/vám líbí Praha? 6. Rozumíš mu? 7. Neviděl jsem tě tam. 8. Dej jim to. 9. Potřebuje něco od nás?

3. 1. vaše 2. mé/mojí 3. náš, naše 4. jejich 5. jeho, její 6. jejich 7. vaše, naše 8. jeho, jejím 9. mou 10. tvůj

4. 1. Znáš jejich adresu? 2. To/toto/tohle je naše první návštěva. 3. Moje žena je učitelka. 4. Vaše pasy, prosím. 5. Je to/toto/tohle jeho kufr? 6. To/toto/tohle je její dům. 7. Tvůj/váš pokoj je ve třetím patře. 8. Můj bratr a jeho sestra chodí na Karlovu universitu. 9. Naše auto je modré. 10. Chci slyšet o jejich dovolené.

5. 1. Nobody knows anything. 2. Is anybody home? 3. I can never find him. 4. Is there a/any restaurant here? 5. I do not have to talk to anybody. 6. I do not have any book. 7. She lives somewhere in Prague.

## Lesson 7.

1. mladě, pilně, zimně, hlavně, anglicky, pražsky, sladce, nově, dlouze/dlouho, úzce/úzko, široce/široko, staře, rychle, silně, dobře, červeně.

2. 1. čekej/ čekejme/ čekejte 2. čti/ čtěmě/ čtěte
3. nespěchej/ nespěchejme/ nespěchejte 4. pracuj/ pracujme/ pracujte

5. mluv/ mluvme/ mluvte 6. nepij 7. napiš 8. kup/ kupte
9. zaplať/ zaplaťme/ zaplaťte

3. 1. vyšší 2. hezčí 3. nejchytřejší 4. rychlejší, nejrychlejší
5. teplejší, nejteplejší 6. dražší 7. nejmilejší 8. lepší
9. nejmenší 10. praktičtější 11. největší

**Lesson 8.**

1. 1. musím 2. musíš 3. chcete 4. smím 5. umíte 6. chtějí se

2. 1. Kdyby jel Petr do Prahy, šel by do kina. 2. Kdybychom byli
doma, poslouchali bychom hudbu. 3. Kdyby mi pomohli, dal bych
jim peníze. 4. Kdybys přišel, dostal bys večeři.
5. Kdybyste mi zavolali, sešli bychom se.

3. 1. Chci, abys to koupil. 2. Chci, abyste mi zavolali. 3. Chci, abys
mi dal tu knihu. 4. Chci, abychom se představili. 5. Chci, abys šel
do kina. 6. Chci, abys na mě čekal před školou.

4. a) čtvrtou        b) devátou
   c) třináctého      d) dvacátém
   e) třetí           f) páté
   g) dvacátého sedmého  h) třicátého prvního
   ch) sedmé         i) druhý

5. vysoký-nízký        chytrý-hloupý
   pracovitý-líný       starý-mladý
   malý-velký           tvrdý-měkký
   sladký-kyselý        těžký-lehký
   otevřený-zavřený     krátký-dlouhý
   čistý-špinavý        hezký-ošklivý

**Lesson 9.**

1. 1. stole 2. universitní knihovně 3. novou studentkou
   4. Národního divadla 5. moderních cizích literaturách
   6. dalekých místech

2. 1. ve 2. před/za 3. u 4. k 5. do 6. k, v, mezi 7. s 8. přes 9. u/vedle 10. před/za 11. vedle, u 12. pod 13. nad

3. 1. Petrova 2. Josefově 3. sestřin 4. Janinou 5. Karlovým 6. sestřině 7. babiččinu 8. Josefova 9. Havlova 10. otcova a matčina

## Lesson 10.

1. Petr píše dopis Mary. Mary bydlí ve Spojených státech. Bydlí ve státě Texas. Chodí tam na universitu. Mary studuje slovanské jazyky. Petr se seznámil s Mary v Praze. Mary tu učila angličtinu.

2. 1. jde, chodí 2. chodím, jdu 3. jdeš 4. chodíš 5. chodí

3. 1. jezdí 2. jedu 3. jezdím 4. jezdím

4. 1. městský 2. pražský 3. studentský 4. třídní 5. učitelský 6. americký 7. lékařský 8. slovní 9. strojní 10. dopisní 11. zimní 12. lesní 13. přírodní 14. mořský

5. 1. Chlapec je nemocen. 2. Petr je hotov. 3. Prosím, buď tak laskav a zavři dveře. 4. Jsem zvědav, jak to dopadne. 5. Jsem velmi spokojen.

# Czech - English Vocabulary

## A
| | |
|---|---|
| aby | in order to 8 |
| adresa | address 5 |
| ale | but 4 |
| alespoň | at least 9 |
| Američan/Američanka | American male/female 1 |
| Amerika | America 1 |
| anglicky | English (adv.) 3 |
| anglický | English (adj.) 3 |
| angličtina | English language 1 |
| ano | yes 1 |
| auto | car 3 |
| autobus | bus 5 |
| až | till, until 5 |

## B
| | |
|---|---|
| babička | grandmother 1 |
| balit/zabalit | to pack 10 |
| banka | bank 1 |
| barva | color 4 |
| běhat/běžet | to run 10 |
| během (prepos., gen.) | during 9 |
| bez (prepos., gen.) | without 2 |
| béžový | beige 7 |
| bílý | white 4 |
| bledý | pale 9 |
| blízko | near (adv.) 5 |
| blízký | near (adj.) 5 |
| bolest (f., kost) | pain 9 |
| bolest hlavy | headache 9 |
| bolestivý | painful 9 |
| bolet (imp.) | to hurt/to have pain 9 |
| bota | shoe 7 |
| brambora | potato 6 |
| bramborový salát | potato salad 6 |

| | |
|---|---|
| brát | to take 3 |
| bratr | brother 6 |
| brzo/brzy | early 9 |
| březen | March 5 |
| břicho | abdomen 9 |
| bunda | jacket 7 |
| bydlet (imp.) | to live, to reside 1 |
| byt | apartment 8 |
| být | to be 1 |

**C**

| | |
|---|---|
| celní kontrola | customs 2 |
| celník | custom officer 2 |
| celý | whole 9 |
| cena | price 4 |
| cesta | way/trip 5 |
| cítit (imp.) | to feel 9 |
| cizí | foreign 5 |
| co | what 1 |

**Č**

| | |
|---|---|
| čaj | tea 6 |
| čas | time /free time 1 |
| časově | timing/timely 10 |
| Čech/Češka | Czech male/female 1 |
| čekat | to wait 1 |
| černý | black 4 |
| červen | June 5 |
| červenec | July 5 |
| červený | red 4 |
| Česká republika | Czech Republic 1 |
| česky | Czech (adv.) 1 |
| český | Czech (adj.) 1 |
| čeština | Czech language 1 |
| číslo | number 4 |
| číst (imp.) | to read 2 |
| čistý | clean 8 |
| číšník/servírka | waiter/waitress 6 |
| člověk/lidé | person/people 3 |
| čokoláda | chocolate 8 |
| čtvrtek | Thursday 5 |
| čtvrtý | fourth 4 |
| čtyři | four 4 |

**D**

| | |
|---|---|
| dál | further 7 |
| daleko | far (adv.) 5 |
| daleký | far (adj.) 5 |
| dárek | gift 2 |
| datum (n., město) | date 5 |
| dávat/dát | to give 3 |
| dávat si/dát si | to have (in terms of food) 6 |
| dcera | daughter 1 |
| dědeček | grandfather 1 |
| děkovat | to thank 1 |
| dělat/udělat | to do 1 |
| den | day 5 |
| déšť | rain 4 |
| dětský pokoj | children's room/bedroom 8 |
| dieta | diet 9 |
| dítě/děti | child/children 1 |
| dívat se/podívat se | to watch/to look 7 |
| dívka/holka | girl 5 |
| dlouho | long (adv.) 2 |
| dlouhý | long (adj.) 7 |
| dnes | today 1 |
| do (prepos., gen.) | to, into, till 2 |
| doba | period 1 |
| dobrý | good (adj.) 3 |
| dobře | good (adv.) 3 |
| doktor/doktorka | doctor male/female 9 |
| doleva | to the left 5 |
| doma (adv.-loc.) | home (adv.) 1 |
| domů (adv.-dir.) | home (adv.) 3 |
| dopis | letter 3 |
| doprava (noun) | transportation/traffic 3 |
| doprava (adv.) | to the right 5 |
| doprovázet to | accompany 1 |
| dostávat/dostat | to get 5 |
| dovážet (imp.) | to import 10 |
| dovést | to be able to/ to know how 8 |
| dovolená | vacation 4 |
| dovolení | permission 9 |
| dovolit | to allow 1 |
| drahý | expensive 7 |
| druhý | second 2 |
| držet (imp.) | to hold 9 |

| | |
|---|---|
| dříve | earlier **8** |
| duben | April **5** |
| dům | house **1** |
| dva/dvě | two **2** |
| dveře (pl.) | door **8** |
| dýchat (imp.) | to breathe **9** |
| džus | juice **6** |

**E**

| | |
|---|---|
| ekonomika | economics **10** |

**F**

| | |
|---|---|
| fialový | purple **4** |
| firma | firm **10** |
| formulář | form **4** |

**G**

| | |
|---|---|
| gin | gin **8** |
| guláš | goulash **6** |

**H**

| | |
|---|---|
| hala | hall **3** |
| halenka | blouse **7** |
| haléř | heller **5** |
| hezký | pretty **7** |
| hlava | head **9** |
| hlávkový salát | lettuce **6** |
| hlavní | main **5** |
| hlavní jídlo | main dish **6** |
| hledat (imp.) | to look for **4** |
| hloupý | dumb, stupid **8** |
| hluboký | deep **7** |
| hned | immediately/right away **5** |
| hnědý | brown **4** |
| hodina | hour/lesson **1** |
| hodně | a lot **3** |
| holičství | barber shop **4** |
| hořký | bitter **9** |
| hospoda | pub/brewery **6** |
| hotel | hotel **4** |
| houska/rohlík | roll **6** |
| hovězí (maso) | beef (meat) **6** |
| hovořit (imp.) | to talk **1** |

| | |
|---|---|
| hrad | castle 2 |
| hrát (imp.) | to play 8 |
| hudba | music 4 |

**CH**

| | |
|---|---|
| chlapec/hoch/kluk | boy 5 |
| chleba | bread 6 |
| chodba | hallway 8 |
| chodec | pedestrian 5 |
| chodit/jít | to go by foot/to attend 2 |
| chtít (imp.) | to want 1 |
| chutnat/ochutnat | to taste 6 |
| chytrý | smart 7 |

**I**

| | |
|---|---|
| inženýr | engineer 1 |

**J**

| | |
|---|---|
| já | I 1 |
| jablko | apple 6 |
| Jaderské moře | Adriatic sea 10 |
| jak | how 1 |
| jaký | what kind/jaký 3 |
| jarní | spring (adj.) 4 |
| jaro | spring (noun) 4 |
| jazyk | language/tongue 3 |
| jeden/jedna/jedno | one 1 |
| jeho | his/its 6 |
| její | her, hers 6 |
| jejich | their, theirs 6 |
| jen/jenom | only 4 |
| jestli | if 7 |
| jet/jezdit | to go (by transportation) 2 |
| jídlo | food 6 |
| jiný | different/other 4 |
| jíst/najíst | to eat 6 |
| jistě | of course 2 |
| jmenovat se (imp.) | to be called 1 |

**K**

| | |
|---|---|
| k, ke (prepos., dat.) | to, toward 3 |
| kabát | coat 4 |
| kabátek | jacket 9 |

| | |
|---|---|
| kabinka | fitting room 7 |
| kadeřnictví | hair dresser/beauty shop 4 |
| kalhoty (pl.) | pants 7 |
| kam | where 3 |
| Karlova universita | Charles University 4 |
| káva | coffee 6 |
| kavárna | coffee house 6 |
| kde | where 1 |
| kdo | who 1 |
| kdy | when 5 |
| kdyby | if 8 |
| kino | movie theater 3 |
| klíč | key 4 |
| knedlík | dumpling 6 |
| kniha | book 2 |
| knihovna | library 2 |
| kočka | cat 8 |
| koláč | fruit cake 8 |
| kolej (f.) | dormitory 2 |
| koleno | knee 9 |
| kolik | how much 5 |
| kolo | bicycle 9 |
| konec | end 4 |
| koruna | crown (Czech currency) 3 |
| kost (f.) | bone 2 |
| košile (f.) | shirt 7 |
| koupelna | bathroom 8 |
| krásně | beautifully 8 |
| krásný | beautiful 7 |
| krátký | short 7 |
| krev (f., kolej) | blood 9 |
| krevní tlak | blood pressure 9 |
| krk | neck 9 |
| krýt (imp.) | to cover 3 |
| křižovatka | intersection 5 |
| který | which one 3 |
| kufr | suitcase 2 |
| kuchyň | kitchen 8 |
| kuchyně | (ethnic) food 8 |
| kupovat/koupit | to buy 3 |
| kuře | chicken 2 |
| květen | May 6 |
| květina | flower 4 |

Beginner's CZECH 153

kyselý — sour 6

**L**

láhev (f. , kolej) — bottle 8
leden — January 6
lehký — light 7
lékař/lékařka — physician male/female 1
lekce (f.) — lesson 1
let — flight 1
letadlo — airplane 1
letecky — by plane/air mail 5
letět (imp.) — to fly 1
letiště — airport 1
letní — summer (adj.) 4
léto — summer (noun) 4
letos — this year 5
líbit se (imp.) — to like 4
lidé/lidi — people 3
lidský — human (adj.) 7
líný — lazy 8
listopad — November 6
literatura — literature 5
litovat (imp.) — to be sorry 6
lodičky (pl.) — dress shoes 7
loni — last year 5
ložnice — bedroom/master bedroom 8
lyžovat (imp.) — to ski 8
lžíce (f.) — spoon 6

**M**

málo — few 4
malý — small 2
manžel/manželka — husband/wife 1
manželský pár — married couple 1
mapa — map 8
máslo — butter 6
maso — meat 6
matka — mother 1
mazat (imp.) — to spread 3
měkký — soft 7
měřit/změřit — to measure 9
měsíc — month/moon 5

| | |
|---|---|
| město | city 2 |
| městský | city (adj.) 5 |
| metr | meter 5 |
| metro | subway 6 |
| mezi (prepos., acc./inst.) | between 3 |
| míchaný | mixed 6 |
| milión | million 5 |
| minout (imp.) | to pass/to miss 3 |
| minuta | minute 5 |
| místní | local 3 |
| místo (noun) | place 1 |
| místo (prepos., gen.) | instead 9 |
| mít (imp.) | to have 1 |
| mladý | young 4 |
| mléko | milk 6 |
| mluvit/promluvit | to speak 1 |
| mnoho | many 3 |
| moc | a lot 6 |
| moci (imp.) | can, to be able to 2 |
| moderní | modern 5 |
| modrý | blue 4 |
| moře | sea 2 |
| most | bridge 2 |
| možná | maybe 5 |
| můj | my, mine 6 |
| muset | must 5 |
| museum or muzeum (n., město) | museum 5 |
| muž | man/husband 1 |
| my | we 1 |
| myslet (imp.) | to think 3 |
| myslet na (acc.) | to think about 3 |

**N**

| | |
|---|---|
| na (prepos., acc./prep.) | on, at 1 |
| na zdraví | to your health/cheers 6 |
| nad (prepos., acc./prep.) | above 9 |
| nádherný | beautiful 8 |
| nacházet/najít (najdu) | to find 6 |
| najít | to find 7 |
| nákup | shopping 7 |
| nalevo | on the left 5 |
| nápad | idea 6 |
| nápoj | drink 6 |

| | |
|---|---|
| napravo | on the right 5 |
| naproti (prepos.,dat.) | opposite to, across from 2 |
| narodit se | to be born 2 |
| národní | national 5 |
| nastupovat/nastoupit | get on 5 |
| náš | our, ours 1 |
| návštěva | visit 1 |
| navštívenka | business card 10 |
| navštívit | to visit 1 |
| ne | no 1 |
| nebo | or 2 |
| něco | something 2 |
| neděle | Sunday 5 |
| nechávat/nechat | to leave sth. 6 |
| nějak | somehow 6 |
| nějaký | some kind of 6 |
| někde | somewhere 6 |
| někdo | somebody 2 |
| někdy | sometime 6 |
| některý | some 6 |
| nemocnice (f.) | hospital 9 |
| nemocný | sick/ill 9 |
| nevolnost (f., kost) | discomfort 9 |
| než | than 7 |
| nic | nothing 6 |
| nijak | in no way 6 |
| nikde | nowhere 6 |
| nikdo | nobody 6 |
| nikdy | never 6 |
| nízký | short 8 |
| noc | night 2 |
| noha | foot/leg 9 |
| normální | normal 9 |
| nos | nose 9 |
| nosit/nést | to carry 3 |
| noviny (pl.) | newspaper 9 |
| nový | new 5 |
| nudle (f., růže) | noodle 8 |
| nula | zero 5 |
| nutný | necessary 10 |
| nůž | knife 6 |
| nyní | now 1 |

# O

| | |
|---|---|
| o (prepos., prep.) | about 2 |
| obal | cover 4 |
| oběd | lunch 6 |
| obědvat | to eat lunch 6 |
| obejít | to go around 9 |
| obchod | store 4 |
| obchodní | department (adj.) 5 |
| obchodní dům | department store 5 |
| objednávat/objednat | to order 4 |
| oblečení | clothes 7 |
| oblek | suit 7 |
| obloha | sky 4 |
| obraz | picture/painting 4 |
| obtížný | difficult 6 |
| obuv | shoes/shoe department 7 |
| obývací pokoj | living room 8 |
| obyvatel | inhabitant 9 |
| od (prepos., gen.) | from 3 |
| odborník | expert 9 |
| oddělení | department (noun) 7 |
| oddělit | to separate 9 |
| odejít | to leave 1 |
| odcházet/odejít | to leave (on foot) 8 |
| odlet | departure (by plane) 8 |
| odlétat (imp.) | to depart (by airplane) 1 |
| odpoledne | afternoon 1 |
| odpověď | answer 5 |
| odpovídat/odpovědět | to answer 5 |
| okamžik | moment 4 |
| okno | window 8 |
| oko/oči | eye/eyes 9 |
| okolo (preps., gen.) | around 9 |
| okurka | cucumber 6 |
| on | he 1 |
| ona | she 1 |
| oni | they 1 |
| ono | it 1 |
| opakovat (imp.) | to repeat 5 |
| oranžový | orange 4 |
| oslava | party/celebration 10 |
| osmý | eighth 8 |
| ošetření | care (medical) 9 |

| | |
|---|---|
| ošetřit | to give care 9 |
| ošklivý | ugly 7 |
| otáčet se (imp.) | to turn around 9 |
| otec | father 1 |
| otevírat/otevřít | to open 2 |
| ovoce | fruit (noun) 6 |
| ovocný | fruit (adj.) 8 |

**P**

| | |
|---|---|
| padnout | to fit, to suit 7 |
| palec | thumb 9 |
| pamatovat si (imp.) | to remember 5 |
| pán | Mr. 1 |
| paní | Mrs. 1 |
| park | park 2 |
| parkování | parking 6 |
| parkovat/zaparkovat | to park 4 |
| parkoviště (n.) | parking lot 4 |
| pas | passport 2 |
| pasová kontrola | passport control 2 |
| pátek | Friday 5 |
| patro | floor (e.g., 3rd floor) 4 |
| pátý | fifth 5 |
| pec (f.) | oven 2 |
| péci | to bake 3 |
| pěkný | nice 2 |
| peníze (pl., stroj) | money 5 |
| pepř | pepper 6 |
| pero | pen 4 |
| pes | dog 8 |
| pěšky | on foot (adv.) 5 |
| pět | five 5 |
| pilný | diligent,hard-working 7 |
| písemný | written 10 |
| pít (imp.) | to drink 6 |
| pití | drink 6 |
| pivo | beer 6 |
| plán | plan 1 |
| platit/zaplatit za (acc.) | to pay for 3 |
| Plzeňský Prazdroj | Pilsner Urquell 6 |
| po (prepos., prep.) | after 9 |
| pobočka | division 10 |
| pobyt | stay 2 |

| | |
|---|---|
| počasí | weather 4 |
| počítač | computer (noun) 1 |
| počítačový | computer (adj.) 1 |
| počítat (imp.) | to count, to compute 8 |
| pod (prepos., acc./inst.) | under/underneath 3 |
| podávat | to serve 4 |
| podepisovat/podepsat | to sign 10 |
| podle | along/according to 5 |
| podnik | company (noun) 10 |
| podnikový | company (adj.) 10 |
| podpis | signature 10 |
| podzemní | underground (adj.) 4 |
| podzim | fall (noun) 4 |
| podzimní | fall (adj.) 4 |
| pohodlný | comfortable/lazy 6 |
| pohostinnost | hospitality 8 |
| pochutnat si | to enjoy (meal) 6 |
| pokládat/položit | to put 9 |
| pokladna | cash register 7 |
| pokoj | room 4 |
| pokračovat | to proceed/to continue 2 |
| pole | field 2 |
| polévka | soup 6 |
| pomáhat/pomoci | to help 7 |
| pomalu | slowly 7 |
| pomalý | slow 7 |
| pomeranč | orange 6 |
| pomerančový džus | orange juice 6 |
| pomoc (f., kost) | help 7 |
| pondělí | Monday 5 |
| pořádek | order 2 |
| posadit se | to sit down/up 9 |
| poschodí | floor (e.g., 3rd floor) 4 |
| posílat/poslat | to send 5 |
| poskytovat/poskytnout | to offer 4 |
| poslouchat (imp.) | to listen 7 |
| pospíchat | to hurry 7 |
| pošta | post office 5 |
| potom | after/then 8 |
| potřebovat (imp.) | to need 3 |
| používat (imp.) | to use 6 |
| pozdě | late (adv.) 8 |
| pozdní | late (adj.) 8 |

| | |
|---|---|
| pozítří | the day after tomorrow 9 |
| poznávat/poznat | to recognize 6 |
| pozvání | invitation 8 |
| práce (f.) | work 1 |
| pracovat (imp.) | to work 1 |
| pracovitý | hard-working 8 |
| Praha | Prague 1 |
| praktický | practical 7 |
| právě | right now 1 |
| pravidelně | regularly 9 |
| pravidelný | regular 9 |
| pro (prepos., acc.) | for 2 |
| problém | problem 8 |
| proclení | declaration 2 |
| projít | to pass through 9 |
| prominout | to forgive 1 |
| prosinec | December 5 |
| prosit/poprosit | to ask for 3 |
| protože | because 8 |
| provoz | traffic 3 |
| prst | finger 9 |
| první | first 1 |
| přát/popřát | to wish 2 |
| přátelé (pl.) | friends 10 |
| přečíst | to finish reading 9 |
| před (prepos.,acc./inst.) | in front of 2 |
| předkrm | appetizer 6 |
| přednáška | lecture 4 |
| předseda (m.) | chairman 2 |
| představovat se/představit se | to introduce oneself 1 |
| přejíst se | to eat too much 8 |
| přejít | to walk across 9 |
| přesunovat/přesunout | to move 8 |
| přesvědčen (short adj.) | convinced 10 |
| přesvědčený | convinced 10 |
| přibližně | approximately 5 |
| přijet | to come (by transportation) 4 |
| přijít | to come (on foot) 6 |
| přijít naproti | to meet 1 |
| přiléhavý | suitable 10 |
| přílet | arrival (by plane) 2 |
| příliš | too much 6 |
| přímo | directly 5 |

| | |
|---|---|
| přinést | to bring 6 |
| připíjet/připít | to toast 6 |
| připravovat/připravit | to prepare 8 |
| příroda | nature 10 |
| příští | next 5 |
| příští rok | next year 5 |
| přítel/přítelkyně | friend male/female 10 |
| přízemí | first floor 4 |
| psát/napsat | to write 3 |
| ptát se/zeptat se | to ask 5 |
| pyžamo | pajama 9 |

**R**

| | |
|---|---|
| rád (short adj.) | to like 4 |
| raději | rather 6 |
| ráno | morning 2 |
| recepce | front desk 4 |
| recepční | front desk clerk 4 |
| republika | republic 1 |
| restaurace (f.) | restaurant 4 |
| roční období | season 4 |
| rodina | family 9 |
| roh | corner 6 |
| rok | year 5 |
| rovně | straight 5 |
| rozdíl | difference 5 |
| rozejít se | to split up, to go separate ways 7 |
| rozhodující | determining 7 |
| rozumět (imp.) | to understand 3 |
| ruka | hand 9 |
| rusky | Russian (adv.) 7 |
| ruský | Russian (adj.) 7 |
| růže (f.) | rose 2 |
| růžový | pink 4 |
| rychlý | fast 6 |
| rýže | rice 6 |

**Ř**

| | |
|---|---|
| řada | row 8 |
| ředitel | director 10 |
| řidič | driver 2 |
| říjen | October 5 |
| říkat/říci | to tell 3 |

| | |
|---|---|
| řízek | (Wiener) schnitzel **6** |
| | |
| **S** | |
| s, se (prepos., inst.) | with **1** |
| sako | sports jacket **7** |
| salát | salad **6** |
| samozřejmě | of course **3** |
| sázet (imp.) | to plant **3** |
| sedět (imp.) | to sit **1** |
| sedmý | seventh **7** |
| sejít se | to meet somewhere with sbd. **9** |
| sestoupit | to go down **9** |
| sestra | sister **6** |
| sešit | notebook **4** |
| setkávat se/setkat se | to meet sbd. **3** |
| seznámení | introduction **1** |
| seznamovat se/seznámit se | to be introduced to/to meet w/sbd. |
| scházet se/sejít se | to meet w/sbd. **3** |
| schodiště (n.) | stairway **4** |
| silný | strong **7** |
| sklenička | glass **6** |
| sklízet/sklidit | to clean **8** |
| sladký | sweet **6** |
| slepičí vývar/polévka | chicken soup **8** |
| slovanský | slavic **10** |
| slovník | dictionary **5** |
| slovo | word **2** |
| slunce (n.) | sun **4** |
| služba | service **4** |
| služební cesta | business trip **1** |
| slyšet/uslyšet | to hear **1** |
| směnárna | money exchange **4** |
| smět | to be allowed to **8** |
| smlouva | agreement **10** |
| snadný | easy **7** |
| snídaně | breakfast **6** |
| snídat | to eat breakfast **4** |
| sníh | snow **4** |
| sobota | Saturday **5** |
| software | software **10** |
| soudce (m.) | judge **2** |
| spěchat (imp.) | to hurry **7** |
| Spojené státy | United States **1** |

| Spojené státy americké | United States of America 1 |
|---|---|
| spojení | connection 10 |
| spojený | connected 8 |
| spokojený | satisfied 6 |
| společenský | formal 10 |
| společnost (f., kost) | society 10 |
| spolu | together 10 |
| spolužák/spolužačka | classmate male/female 9 |
| spropitné | tip 6 |
| srdce (n.) | heart 9 |
| srpen | August 5 |
| stanoviště | stop (noun) 3 |
| starý | old 4 |
| stát | to cost 5 |
| stát/zastavit | to stop/to stand 9 |
| stav | condition (medical) 9 |
| stávat se/stát se | to happen 8 |
| stavení | building 2 |
| stihnout | to make it on time 7 |
| sto | hundred 5 |
| století | century 5 |
| stroj | machine 2 |
| strom | tree 4 |
| strýc | uncle 9 |
| středa | Wednesday 5 |
| stříbrný | silver 4 |
| student/studentka | student male/female 2 |
| studený | cold 7 |
| studovat (imp.) | to study 3 |
| stůl | table 2 |
| suchý | dry 9 |
| sukně (f.) | skirt 4 |
| sůl | salt 6 |
| suterén | basement 4 |
| suvenýr | souvenir 4 |
| svačina | snack 6 |
| sval | muscle 9 |
| světle | light (adv.) 7 |
| světlý | light (adj.) 7 |
| svetr | sweater 4 |
| svíčková pečeně | sirloin of beef 6 |
| svlékat se/svléknout se | to take off clothes 9 |
| sympatický | likable, nice 3 |

| | |
|---|---|
| syn | son 1 |

**Š**

| | |
|---|---|
| šampaňské (víno) | champagne (wine) 8 |
| šaty (pl.) | dress 7 |
| šedý | grey 4 |
| šestý | sixth 6 |
| široký | wide 7 |
| škola | school 1 |
| špatný | bad 6 |
| špinavý | dirty 8 |
| štěstí | luck 3 |

**T**

| | |
|---|---|
| tady | here 1 |
| také | also 1 |
| taky | also 8 |
| talíř | plate 6 |
| tam | over there 2 |
| tamhle | over there 7 |
| tamten | that (one) 4 |
| taxametr | meter 3 |
| taxi | taxi 3 |
| telefon | telephone 4 |
| telefonicky | by telephone 4 |
| telefonní | telephone (adj.) 10 |
| tělo | body 9 |
| tělocvična | exercise room 4 |
| téměř/skoro | almost 6 |
| ten/ta/to | that 4 |
| tenhle | this (one) 4 |
| teplota | temperature 9 |
| těšit se | to look forward to 1 |
| teta | aunt 9 |
| těžký | heavy/difficult 7 |
| tichý | quiet 7 |
| tisíc | thousand 5 |
| tisknout/natisknout | to print 3 |
| to | it, that, this 1 |
| tonik | tonic (water) 8 |
| tradice | tradition 8 |
| tradiční | traditional 8 |
| tramvaj (f.) | streetcar 5 |

| | |
|---|---|
| tráva | grass 4 |
| trh | market 10 |
| tričko | T-shirt 7 |
| trochu | little bit 8 |
| trpět (imp.) | to suffer 3 |
| třetí | third 3 |
| tři | three 3 |
| třída | class/classroom 5 |
| tvrdý | hard 7 |
| tvůj | your, yours 6 |
| týden | week 2 |

**U**

| | |
|---|---|
| u (prepos., gen.) | by 2 |
| ubytování | lodging, accommodations 4 |
| účet | bill 3 |
| učit/naučit | to teach/learn 1 |
| učitel/učitelka | teacher male/female 1 |
| ucho/uši | ear/ears 9 |
| ukazovat/ukázat | to show 3 |
| ulice | street 3 |
| umět | to know how 8 |
| umřít | to die 3 |
| universita or univerzita | university 4 |
| únor | February 5 |
| určitě | surely 1 |
| úředník/úřednice | clerk male/female 5 |
| ústa (pl.) | mouth 9 |
| úterý | Tuesday 5 |
| úzký | narrow 7 |
| už/již | already 8 |
| užívat/používat | to use 6 |

**V**

| | |
|---|---|
| v, ve (prepos.,acc./prep.) | in 1 |
| vadit | to hamper, to matter 3 |
| váha | weight/scale 5 |
| vařit/uvařit | to cook 6 |
| váš | your, yours (pl.) 4 |
| včera | yesterday (adv.) 5 |
| večeře | dinner 6 |
| večeřet | to eat dinner 6 |

| | |
|---|---|
| večírek | party/(social) event 10 |
| věda | science 2 |
| vědět (imp.) | to know sth. 3 |
| vedle (prepos., gen.) | next to 1 |
| velikost (f., kost) | size 7 |
| velký | big 2 |
| velmi | very 3 |
| vepřové (maso) | pork (meat) 6 |
| veřejný | public 5 |
| věta | sentence, clause 8 |
| vidět/uvidět | to see 1 |
| vidlička | fork 6 |
| vinárna | wine cellar 6 |
| víno | wine 6 |
| viset (imp.) | to hang 9 |
| vlak | train 5 |
| vlasy (pl.) | hair 9 |
| vlevo | on the left 4 |
| voda | water 6 |
| vodit/vést | to lead, to take 10 |
| volat/zavolat | to call/to telephone 4 |
| vonět (imp.) | to smell(good) 8 |
| vozit/vézt | to carry/to transport 2 |
| vpravo | on the right 4 |
| vracet/vrátit | to return 7 |
| vrchní | head waiter 6 |
| vstávat/vstát | to get up 10 |
| vstoupit | to enter 9 |
| všechen (pron.) | all 7 |
| všechno | all 2 |
| vy | you (pl.) 1 |
| vybavení | equipment 9 |
| vybírat si/vybrat si | to choose/to select 6 |
| výborný | delicious/excellent 6 |
| vyhovovat/vyhovět | to satisfy/to suit/to accommodate 6 |
| vyjít | to start walking 9 |
| vyjíždět/vyjet | to drive out, to leave 8 |
| výlet | trip 4 |
| vypadat | to look like 9 |
| vyplnit | to fill in/out 4 |
| vyrábět (imp.) | to produce, to make 10 |
| vyřídit | to take care of sth. 10 |
| vyřízený | taken care of 10 |

| | |
|---|---|
| vysoký | tall **7** |
| vystavovat/vystavit | to display **7** |
| vystoupit | to get off **9** |
| vystupovat/vystoupit | to get off **5** |
| výtah | elevator **4** |
| vyvážet/vyvézt | to export **10** |
| vyzkoušet | to try (on) **7**/ |
| | to test **10** |
| vyzvednout | to pick-up, to get **2** |
| vzduch | air **9** |

**Z**

| | |
|---|---|
| z, ze (prepos., gen.) | from **2** |
| za (prepos.,acc./inst.) | behind, in back of **2** |
| začátek | beginning **4** |
| začínat/začnout | to begin, to start **3** |
| záda | back **9** |
| zahrnutý | included **4** |
| zahýbat/zahnout | to turn **5** |
| záchod | toilet, rest room **8** |
| zajímat se o (acc.) | to be interested in **5** |
| základní | basic **1** |
| základní škola | elementary school **1** |
| zákusek | dessert **6** |
| záležitost (f., kost) | affair (business matter) **10** |
| zámek | chateaux/lock **2** |
| zaměstnání | employment/work/job **1** |
| zamlouvat/zamluvit | to make reservation, to reserve **6** |
| září | September **5** |
| zastávka | stop (noun) **5** |
| zastavovat/zastavit | to stop **3** |
| zatelefonovat | to call, to telephone **4** |
| zavazadlo | luggage **2** |
| zavírat/zavřít | to close **7** |
| závrať (f., kost) | dizziness **9** |
| zde, tu | here **2** |
| zdraví (noun) | health **9** |
| zdravý | healthy **9** |
| zdravotní | medical **9** |
| zelenina | vegetable **6** |
| zelený | green **4** |
| zelí | sauerkraut **6** |
| země (f.) | country/earth/the Earth **8** |

| | |
|---|---|
| zhoršovat/zhoršit | to get worse 9 |
| zima | winter (noun) 4 |
| zimní | winter (adj.) 4 |
| zítra | tomorrow (adv.) 5 |
| zkoušet/zkusit | to try 7 |
| zkušenost (f., kost) | experience 4 |
| zlatý | gold (adj.) 4 |
| změnit se | to change 6 |
| známí (noun, pl.) | friends 9 |
| známý (noun, sing.) | friend 9 |
| známý (adj.) | known/familiar 1 |
| znát/poznat | to know sbd./to recognize sth. 3 |
| znít | to sound 8 |
| zub | tooth 9 |
| zůstávat/zůstat | to stay 10 |
| zvát/pozvat | to invite 8 |
| zvonek | bell 8 |
| zvonit/zazvonit | to ring 8 |
| zvykat si/zvyknout si | to get used to 9 |
| zvyklý | accustomed 9 |
| zvýšená teplota | higher temperature 9 |
| zvýšený | higher 9 |

## Ž

| | |
|---|---|
| žádný | none 6 |
| žaludeční | stomach (adj.) 9 |
| žaludek | stomach (noun) 9 |
| že | that 3 |
| žena | wife 1 |
| židle (f.) | chair 4 |
| žít (imp.) | to live 1 |
| žlutý | yellow 4 |

# Audio Track List

 Audio files available at:
**http://www.hippocrenebooks.com/beginners-online-audio.html**

**FOLDER ONE**
1. Title—Beginner's Czech
2. The Czech Alphabet
3. Short Vowels
4. Long Vowels
5. Hard Vowels and Soft Vowels
6. Hard Consonants
7. Soft Consonants
8. Neutral Consonants
9. Voiced and Voiceless Consonants
10. Neutralization of Final Consonants
11. Assimilation of Consonants
12. Lesson 1 Dialogue
13. Lesson 1 Dialogue for repetition
14. Lesson 1 Vocabulary
15. Lesson 1 Expressions
16. Lesson 2 Dialogue
17. Lesson 2 Dialogue for repetition
18. Lesson 2 Vocabulary
19. Lesson 3 Dialogue
20. Lesson 3 Dialogue for repetition
21. Lesson 3 Vocabulary
22. Lesson 3 Expressions
23. Lesson 4 Dialogue
24. Lesson 4 Dialogue for repetition
25. Lesson 4 Vocabulary
26. Lesson 4 Colors
27. Lesson 4 Seasons
28. Lesson 5 Dialogue One
29. Lesson 5 Dialogue One for repetition
30. Lesson 5 Dialogue Two
31. Lesson 5 Dialogue Two for repetition
32. Lesson 5 Vocabulary

32. Lesson 5 Vocabulary
33. Lesson 5 Expressions
34. Lesson 5 Cardinal Numbers
35. Lesson 5 Time
36. Lesson 5 Days of the Week
37. Lesson 5 Months of the Year

**FOLDER TWO**
1. Lesson 6 Dialogue One
2. Lesson 6 Dialogue One for repetition
3. Lesson 6 Dialogue Two
4. Lesson 6 Dialogue Two for repetition
5. Lesson 6 Vocabulary
6. Lesson 6 Expressions
7. Lesson 7 Dialogue One
8. Lesson 7 Dialogue One for repetition
9. Lesson 7 Dialogue Two
10. Lesson 7 Dialogue Two for repetition
11. Lesson 7 Vocabulary
12. Lesson 7 Expressions
13. Lesson 8 Dialogue One
14. Lesson 8 Dialogue One for repetition
15. Lesson 8 Dialogue Two
16. Lesson 8 Dialogue Two for repetition
17. Lesson 8 Dialogue Three
18. Lesson 8 Dialogue Three for repetition
19. Lesson 8 Dialogue Four
20. Lesson 8 Dialogue Four for repetition
21. Lesson 8 Vocabulary
22. Lesson 8 Expressions
23. Lesson 8 Ordinal Numbers
24. Lesson 9 Dialogue
25. Lesson 9 Dialogue for repetition
26. Lesson 9 Vocabulary
27. Lesson 9 Expressions
28. Lesson 10 Dialogue
29. Lesson 10 Dialogue for repetition
30. Lesson 10 Vocabulary
31. Lesson 10 Expressions

www.ingramcontent.com/pod-product-compliance
Lightning Source LLC
Jackson TN
JSHW011402130125
77033JS00023B/804

* 9 7 8 0 7 8 1 8 1 4 2 4 9 *